AM I STILL A CHRISTIAN?

Gordon Jeff is Chaplain to St Michael's Anglican Convent, Ham Common, having had thirty years of parochial experience. In 1980 he became a founder member and first Chairman of SPIDIR, an informal network for all concerned in the furtherance of spiritual direction. He has been a pioneer in the development of parish-based retreats, has been much involved in counselling and was formerly a hospital administrator. He is married, with two grown-up children.

Am I still a Christian?

20 QUESTIONS ABOUT YOUR SPIRITUAL DIRECTION

GORDON JEFF

TRI△NGLE

First published 1992
Triangle
SPCK
Holy Trinity Church
Marylebone Road
London NW1 4DU

British Library Cataloguing in Publication Data
A catalogue record for this book is available from the
British Library.

ISBN 0–281–04569–0

Typeset by Inforum Typesetting, Portsmouth
Printed in Great Britain by
BPCC Hazell Books
Aylesbury, Bucks, England
Member of BPCC Ltd.

Contents

Abbreviations for Bible versions

AV	Authorised Version
NJB	New Jerusalem Bible
NEB	New English Bible
NRSV	New Revised Standard Version
ASB	*Alternative Service Book 1980*

Introduction

There are some people who, when told about the traditional Christian faith, appear to be able to accept it all without difficulty. 'If God is God, then who am I to question the Bible or the collective wisdom of the church?' might be one way of putting it.

That is fine up to a point, but I think I should want to know how far such a person has really worked at relating their *experience* of God and of life to the faith they are accepting without question, because unless we are constantly relating our beliefs to our experience of life we may find ourselves putting belief into one watertight compartment and real life into another. Even more seriously, there is a danger of experiencing a major crisis of faith if severe personal tragedy strikes and that person has never tussled with what is really true for them.

Belief, as I understand it, needs constant testing against the hard reality of experience. In any case, what the church believes is not quite as united and monolithic as some might wish to think. So after thirty years of predominantly parochial ministry, during which rather a lot of clergy and laity have come to talk to me in some depth about their Christian journey, I know that there must be a far greater number of Christians carrying with them many questions about what they believe.

Those who come from a more rigid area of the church may feel reluctant even to articulate such questioning. They may feel guilty, as if it is somehow wrong to raise questions: that questions and doubt are somehow 'sinful'. Others find themselves asking, 'If I doubt this or that aspect of belief, can I

1

still be a Christian?' or 'Holding the views I do, or having such an experience of life, can I still be counted a Christian?' or 'If I allow myself to doubt *that* aspect of Christian belief I might find I'm on the path to losing *everything*'.

So this little book is written partly to address the kind of questions the reader may be struggling with. It is a good beginning if we can put aside all those feelings of guilt about such a struggle. It is far better to regard it as normal and as healthy and constructive if we have to struggle with our belief. The book of Job, surely one of the most profound in the Old Testament, is about precisely such a tussle with belief and trust.

Secondly, we do not have to be official ministers in the church to find ourselves confronted by people asking us questions because they know we are Christians. Those who ask us may be Christians themselves or they may be interested enquirers. Their questions may be to do with belief or conduct; they may express doubt, guilt or anger. Anger is most frequently to do with incomprehension at all the suffering in the world which does not easily square with the concept of a loving God. If you are known to be a Christian you may sometimes find others projecting on to you the anger they are really feeling towards God although they may not be angry with you personally. This is a common experience for clergy.

Christians – thoughtful, lifelong Christians – are frequently thrown off-balance by such questions, feeling inadequate to respond to them. Even clergy, as I know from the experience of running courses in spiritual direction, quite often find themselves floundering to find an adequate response.

This is not to imply that we should all have wonderful ready-made 'answers' to which we can refer at a moment's notice, nor would I myself pretend in any way to have all the answers. We probably have tentative ideas about how to respond to questions, but that does not necessarily mean that the way *I* see something will be convincing to another person. They may have already considered the response which satisfies me and have found it wanting for themselves. There are, however, effective or less effective ways of responding to the questions other people ask, and this book is in a very simple way also about Christian listening, or even about what some of us call, until a better term can be generally agreed, 'spiritual direction'.

As we shall see, people need to discover for themselves answers that are true for *them*. Very often the best way of proceeding is not to attempt to provide answers but to encourage people to ponder and pray more deeply about the questions they are asking. I believe that in a very real sense God does help us to resolve our questions when we are ready for it.

I suppose the book has a third purpose. I, too, am on a journey *to* God and on a journey *with* God. These questions are also *my* questions, questions with which I, too, continue to struggle; it is inevitable that at times something of my own journey will become apparent.

So here are twenty questions which I hope will cover quite a lot of ground. There could have been dozens of others; but I feel that the important thing is not to have answers, which in this world are bound to be provisional, but rather to have a healthy *attitude* to the great questions of life and death, good and evil, of pain and pleasure which confront every single person. Right attitudes are more important than right answers because right attitudes allow us the humility of not-knowing, and not-knowing is something to do with worship and with the holiness of God.

The late Anthony de Mello tells the story of a young archer who performed brilliantly at an archery contest. All applauded him except his master, who remained unimpressed. When the pupil asked him why, the master replied, 'You have yet to learn that the target is not the target', and he refused to tell the young man what the true target was. De Mello comments that what he was meant to aim at was not achievement but attitude.[1]

We are all different and some find it harder to live with questions than others; some people will look for more certainty and structure than others, and it is precisley *in* that structure that they find their freedom. The most fitting text for those who actively like a clear structure within which to live and move and have their being could be 'in his service is perfect freedom'.

Others feel fettered by structures of belief and are content to have a small number of near-certainties and to remain open to all the rest. A week before he died, the New Testament scholar J.B. Lightfoot wrote:

> I find my faith suffers nothing by leaving a thousand questions open, so long as I am convinced on two or three main lines . . . Things that edify others do not edify me. I feed upon four or five great ideas.

The more we come to realise the vastness of the universe, so much more immense than the universe as it was understood by biblical writers, the more I believe that we need to live with just a few 'things which are unshaken',[2] with the rest of Christian orthodoxy there to help us, as far as we are at present able to be responsive to it. It was Archbishop William Temple who once wrote, 'Hold fast to Christ, and for the rest be totally uncommited', but for some people even that may raise an awful lot of questions!

There is a well-known story told of the Desert Fathers where a peasant came to the great St Antony and asked Antony to teach him how to pray. So Antony taught him the first verse of the first psalm and told him to go away and ponder it:

Blessed is the man who has not walked in the counsel of
the ungodly; nor followed the way of sinners nor taken his
seat amongst the scornful. (ASB)

'When you have learned what that verse has to say, come
back, and I will teach you more', said Antony. The months,
indeed, the years went by and Antony assumed that the
peasant had given up trying to pray until one day he chanced
to meet him. 'I'm sorry you didn't go on trying to pray,' said
Antony. 'But I did', said the peasant. 'I'm still getting new
meaning from the verse, and when I'm ready I'll come back
to you for more.'

It is becoming clear, in the light of recent scholarship,[3] that
early Christianity was far more varied than has often been
imagined. As we go back into history it is simply not true that
there was once a single simple faith held by all Christians.
Even within the gospels there is variety. One of the exciting
things about talking to people is to find them coming through
a period of doubt and questioning about Jesus into a new
understanding of him without the massive overlay imposed by
the church over the centuries. The early Christians were called
Followers of The Way – a Way based upon their understanding of Jesus. They were not initially required to subscribe to a
checklist of doctrinal points; rather they had seen in Jesus a
way of living which led to a fuller life both for themselves and
others. That remains as true today as it was 2,000 years ago.

So how do we begin?

Essentially I think there are two ways of 'doing theology';
either as a jigsaw puzzle or as a game of dominoes. There are
the systematic theologians (e.g. Aquinas, Barth, Tillich) who
will build up a structure of belief so that at the end of the day
there will be a beautiful picture, with each piece relating to all
the other pieces. Provided we are ready to realise that there will
always be a few gaps, a few pieces which do not fit, or a few

pieces left over, that is fine. The gaps and the bits left over are important and constitute something of the mystery of God.

The other way of 'doing theology' is to regard it more as a game of dominoes; here are are a number of lines of thought, all leading in different directions, but which all make sense from our experience of life, and which are all worth pursuing. That, too, is fine, provided that all the lines of thought are seen to be part of the same game so that in the mystery of God the game somehow holds together.

I have also been greatly helped in thinking about belief by the work done a few years ago in the USA by Bruce Rahtjen and others on another way of looking at theology.[4] To put it briefly, many people think of theology in a manner which Rahtjen calls 'dogmatic theology'. With this model the underlying question is, 'Is is *true?*', so that a doctrine is either true or false, right or wrong. It is a somewhat confrontational approach since doctrines believed to be false will either be opposed or at least ignored. There is little room in the middle for those grey areas which make up so large a part of life. With this approach things tend to be black or white, good or bad.

So who decides which is true and which is false? In dogmatic theology it is the *church*, thus making the *hierarchy* of the church the defenders of the truth.

However, where the authority of a church is questioned, dogmatic theology may to some extent give way to what Rahtjen calls 'systematic theology'. In systematic theology Rahtjen suggests that the underlying question is not so much 'Is this doctrine *true?*', but rather, 'Is it *consistent*, is it coherent with other beliefs and doctrines?' This is very much the jigsaw puzzle approach.

It is easy to see that systematic theology is less confrontational than dogmatic theology, and systematic theologians are more likely to debate with their opponents than to attack them as false.

So who in this instance decides whether the theology is respectable? No longer the hierarchy of the church but now the professional theologians.

But Rahtjen suggests that there is a third way of doing theology which may come about in reaction to the power of the professional theologian. People sometimes think, rightly or wrongly, that academic theologians are rather remote from the everyday world of Monday morning. This third way of doing theology he calls *experiential* theology, in which the main question asked of a belief is, 'Is is *real*?', i.e. 'does this doctrine square with reality as *I* experience reality?'

This means that to the extent that our theology is an experiential theology the important person is neither the church nor the professional theologian, but the believer who tests out the belief against experience. We may not all be theologians, but everyone has a theology!

All three methods have a value and obviously there is much overlap, but I think it is helpful when we talk to people to try to understand whether they are asking if something is true, or whether it forms part of a coherent whole as they look at life, or whether their experience of life really does square with some proclaimed aspect of belief. We also need to know which question we are asking of ourselves. It is my experience that when people come to talk to me they may or may not be interested in orthodox doctrine as propounded in the creeds; they may or may not be interested in the differing ideas of the theologians, but they will all be concerned about trying to understand their own experience of life.

People seldom want pat 'answers'; they really want help in working out how they understand their own lives and their own experience of God. So the more dogmatic, systematic and experiential theology we know the better, but we do not have to be a Thomas Aquinas in order to help people on their journey with and to God. The ability to listen, the ability to ask questions and the ability to love are far more important.[5]

With all this in mind, let's now look at some of the questions frequently asked by Christians and others who are concerned about where their experience of life and of God is taking them. Firstly, what do *you* think about the questions? Secondly, how would you respond if you were asked them by someone else? And I hope that you would try to get behind the questions rather than always attempting to give your own answers, which might not be helpful to another person. And thirdly, on the way you will probably pick up my point that these questions are a few of the many with which I, too, continue to wrestle as I try to understand something of the mystery and the love of God.

If I thought that what I was trying to do was to set up twenty advanced examination questions and then in some imagined wisdom propound 'solutions' in a few paragraphs, I should not even have started. What follows is more a humble experience in exploring how we might most helpfully react when others confront us with such questions. By going beneath the surface we can perhaps begin to see what may lie behind the question.

Let's have a text with us on our journey together:

The truth shall make you free.[6]

References

1. Anthony De Mello, *The Prayer of the Frog* (Prakash, India 1989)
2. Hebrews 12.27 (AV)
3. See, for example, Robert L. Wilken, *The Myth of Christian Beginnings* (SCM 1979); Elaine Pagels, *The Gnostic Gospels* (New York 1979) and *Adam, Eve and the Serpent* (Weidenfeld and Nicolson 1988)
4. Bruce D. Rahtjen, *A Workbook in Experiential Theology* (Associates in Experiential Theology, Inc. 1977)
5. I have developed this line of thought in my earlier book: *Spiritual Direction for Every Christian* (SPCK 1987, 1989, 1991)
6. John 8.32 (AV)

Part One

QUESTIONS
ABOUT BELIEF

Do I have to accept everything Christians are meant to believe?

I wonder what might lie behind that question? It's not a very specific question but a very generalised one, so I think it needs a bit of unravelling.

An inner-city doctor who used to look after my family once said to me that he believed two-thirds of the patients who came to his surgery were really suffering not so much from the physical symptoms they presented to him as from stress or other psychological problems.

Not all his patients would have realised this was their real complaint, and those who did would probably have considered that when you went to a general practitioner you would be expected to present a physical symptom rather than a psychological one. But their underlying dis-ease was rather different, and being a good doctor, although severely overworked in the inner city, he would try in the very limited time at his disposal to go a little deeper.

In much the same way, someone raising a question with a Christian minister or a lay person known to be a Christian would be likely to start with something to do with belief or conduct, because they would consider this to be the kind of question one would be expected to raise with such a person, even if what was truly bothering them was something different.

Some years ago I was involved with a colleague in what was presented to us as anxiety over an allegedly haunted house. It was only as we spent time and listening space that talk of a haunted house receded into the background and finally disappeared and we were left with what was essentially a matter of family relationships. People bring to us what they expect us to be ready to hear. It would have been only too easy to go into the third-rate movie stuff of exorcisms and all that, but this was not what it was really about and would assuredly have done more harm than good.

I can think of any number of needs which might lie behind a question about accepting everything Christians believe. Twice a day, seven days a week, 365 days a year, at the convent where I spend some of my time as chaplain, free meals are provided without question to all needy people who appear. That very necessary act of charity looks after part of their basic physical needs which are no longer adequately covered by social security. But most of them are desperately lonely and not infrequently I find them asking me questions about Christian belief. I don't honestly think that is what their question is really about. They far more urgently need friendship and companionship, but a question about belief is clearly thought to be a valid way of holding my time and attention for a while. They are very lonely people and I know that I do not even begin to respond to them as they deserve. But what is pathetically true of them is equally true of others in less dire straits who may also be in need of attention and friendship. In the final analysis they need someone to give them time, time to listen to their story and to indicate by that gift of time that they matter as people. And that is a very Christian task even if God is not named.

Every one of us has a story to tell, but few are ready to listen to our story. Even fewer are prepared to help us talk at some depth and to relate our own story to some kind of consistent worldview (which is an exercise in our second model of theology, 'systematic theology'). The question with which we began this chapter suggests to me that the speaker could well be in a muddle – one part of his or her life does not really relate to other parts, and orthodox Christianity does not seem to have much relevance to their experience of life. This applies equally to many people in established situations in life and not only to those wayfarers at the convent.

When people begin to think about the meaning and purpose of their life, they often find that they have very few resources to fall back on. They may have developed their thinking in many areas of life to a very sophisticated level, yet their idea of Christianity has progressed no further than a Sunday School level. Sunday School teaching is fine (sometimes!) for Sunday School children, but it is inadequate for grown women and men. So that when people query aspects of Christian belief I think we shall do well first of all, before even attempting to 'answer' their 'objections', to try to find out just what they think Christian beliefs really are.

I find it depressing as I read secular journals to realise the sheer ignorance of Christianity displayed by many clever people who would be ashamed to be so ignorant of art and literature, history or current affairs. Sometimes to caricature Christianity is a convenient defence against having to face the challenge of a credible faith. It may be a comfortable defence against doing some hard thinking if we pretend that *all* Christians subscribe to the narrow life-denying beliefs of the more extreme versions of Christianity.

It is frequently a great relief (sometimes met almost with *dis*-belief) for people to realise that there are countless Christians whose interpretation of Christianity is life-affirming rather than life-denying. They are not always saying 'no' to everything that is pleasurable, and they see something of God in the natural world, in music, art, and poetry, in love-making and in enjoying a good meal with friends. After all, the Last Supper was not the only supper. Indeed, his enemies described Jesus as a glutton and a wine-bibber. I am sure he was neither of those, but the jibe would suggest he was not only the man of sorrows, but also the man of fun and friendship whom people loved to have around.

It is a cliché to say that Christianity is caught, not taught, but I believe that there are Christians around in the world who draw others to what they believe by their own infectious enthusiasm and sense of fun, undergirded by a profound belief that they themselves are loved by God, by a profound belief that they – and everyone – matter as people and that we are ultimately called to a joy that goes beyond anything we can imagine. 'I have said these things to you', declared Jesus, 'so that my joy may be in you and that your joy may be complete.'[1]

So people who come to talk to us may be making challenging statements either in order to draw attention to the fact that they want to tell their story to another person, or because they want to get their lives into some kind of order and purpose; they may have been trying for years to have a serious conversation with someone about things that really matter. It may also be that they have a totally distorted idea of Christianity and have formed a view of all Christians from some of those dreadful doorstep conversations with Jehovah's Witnesses or similar extremists.

If none of this seems to be what the questioner really wants to talk about then we need to be more specific. What particular aspects of Christian belief are found to be so difficult? Has any specific event in that person's life brought them to such questioning? Are there emotional or relational problems which have brought them to an attitude of questioning, darkness or even despair? At a juncture like this we shall simply be listening to the other person's story, and we may find ourselves closer to counselling than to a discussion of belief. It may be more important to begin by talking about feelings and everyday life situations. God can sometimes be used as a way of evading difficult feelings and questions which are primarily to do with human relationships.

God does not always have to be named in order to be present. I think that to name God in a situation sometimes diminishes both God and the reality of the situation being discussed. It is salutary to recall that the Jews of the Old Testament did not presume even to name God. So much so that they actually forgot the pronunciation of the name and later centuries came to think of 'Jehovah' when it was probably 'Yahweh'. God is present when we are relating in concern and love with another person even if his name is not mentioned.

These, then, are a few of the underlying possibilities behind this initial question, but at the end of the day we may indeed be faced with someone saying, 'Nowadays there's a lot of Christian teaching which I can't accept.' We might then try to ask that person to be more specific so as to narrow down the area of discussion to manageable proportions. That person may never hitherto have done more than state a generalised position of protest. To concentrate the area of discussion will help, and it may be centred on one or more of the questions which come later in this book. They may need to express anger against the way the world (or God) has treated them. Very often the opportunity to express anger or resentment without the listener attempting to justify God's ways or argue the person out of the anger can gradually lead, with the releasing of pressure, to a recognition of many positive facts in their experience. They simply need somewhere to explode.

Any discussion ends well if it can conclude on a positive note. While acknowledging the negative aspect of life, what are the things this person *can* hold on to as real for them? What have been the high spots in their life? These will not necessarily be narrowly 'religious' moments, but times of joy or beauty or insight or fun or being loved. Where might God have been in those high spots? What might have been being communicated to them on those occasions which affirmed them and made them feel valued? We do well to help people to value and understand the high spots in their lives even if at first they find it hard to believe these have anything to do with God as they perceive God. Maybe their concept of God is waiting to be greatly enlarged.

Clergy traditionally stand at the door of the church to say goodbye to people as they go out. Either there or later over coffee people will sometimes grumble about aspects of the service they have just attended and which they disliked (not everyone does this – many are affirming!). They did not like the sermon or a hymn or the prayers, the choir or whatever. I often try to counter this by asking them what they did like or what they did find helpful. We are all different and if there is only one thing in a service which speaks to us, that may be what God is trying to say to us that day. We need to be tolerant and to realise that other people who are very different from ourselves may have found other parts of the service spoke to them. One part was special for me: other parts were special for other people.

It is much the same with what we believe – not at first to dwell too much on what we find hard, but to work on maybe only one or two things which do make sense. The other bits may make sense to us later.

It is a great improvement that the new form of the creed used today by most Christians begins not 'I believe', but 'We believe'. I may not myself be able to believe this part or that part at the moment, perhaps I never shall, but other Christians do believe those parts and find them helpful.

I am told that on a course for training future clergy the students decided at one Eucharist to say the creed very slowly, to stand up for the clauses that they could personally affirm and to sit down for the clauses which they could not personally take on board at that stage. They found it an encouraging experience to notice that at no stage was everybody sitting down! The creed may not be where I happen personally to be at the moment, but the collective faith of the church as a whole.

So we take on board what we can and build upon it, and wait patiently in the hope that other parts may become clearer to us as we proceed in our lives.

And if they do not . . . is that so very dreadful?

Reference

1. John 15.11 (NRSV)

Do I have to believe everything I read in the Bible?

More than in any other section of this little book do I feel a sense of near-lunacy in having posed twenty really major questions to look at in so small a compass! I can only remind myself that we are here not attempting to *answer* questions, but to look at approaches to them. Nor do I, in this chapter, wish to leave the reader with the belief that I devalue the Bible: I do not. One thing I am deeply convinced about is that the many people who have difficulties over the Bible should be encouraged still to continue to consider themselves to be Christians. It is far better to try to validate what they *can* believe than to press them beyond what they can understand at the moment or to bludgeon them into some idea of biblical infallibility.

Clergy and others who have been through theological training are less likely to experience difficulty with the interpretation of the Bible for the simple reason that they will have learned that there are many different ways in which we can understand the Bible and they will also have widely varying views on how the authority of the Bible is to be understood.

One difficulty with the Bible which clergy in particular bring to me is that of boredom. They have read some passages innumerable times and as they read the same one yet again it remains as flat as a pancake stuck there on the page. It becomes even worse if they are trying to prepare a sermon on that passage. Worse still is the guilt which descends on them when they hear of other clergy and laity for whom (apparently) every time they open the Bible the page leaps up at them and everything is wonderful and fresh, new and exciting.

My sceptical self sometimes wonders whether it really is like that for anyone all the time, or whether such people are afraid to acknowledge to others, or perhaps even to themselves, that at times they find the Bible boring. If the whole of their faith is based on the Bible it must be very alarming if the book fails to come alive for them.

Leaving aside that question of not facing honestly the reality of the situation I think there really are two kinds of people here. For some, a Bible story or some other passage is like a greatly loved friend. Each time we visit that friend we remember earlier happy times we have enjoyed together and we look forward to the next visit when we shall learn more of each other and share more experiences together, so that the relationship is continually deepening. For some, the Bible is clearly like that – the delight lies in learning more about the already familiar.

For others the excitement and challenge lie in what is new. It is new ideas and new experiences which bring such people to life. Their prayer, (and their sermon preparation, if they are ministers) will therefore be better if they begin not with the Bible, but with experiences and reflections upon real life 'out there in the world'. The surprising thing is how frequently that new experience will bring us back to a Bible passage which is now lit up for us in an entirely new way – 'so *that's* what the parable was about', or 'I never realised *that* was what Jesus was really talking about'. The Bible has become new and fresh in a way which would not have happened had we taken the Bible as our starting point; to each kind of person the Bible is equally valuable, though in a different way.

19

For this second group of people, Bible reading will almost certainly be more meaningful if they take only a short sentence or phrase and live with it during their prayer time and at other times in the day. What might be called the attributes of God make the starting point for a lifetime of Bible-based prayer. There are many phrases in the Bible to do with the love, joy, peace, wisdom and power of God, for example:

These things have I spoken to you that my joy might remain in you. (AV)

Abide in my love. (AV)

My peace I give to you. (NRSV)

All power is given unto me. (AV)

These may well be shortened, as we pray them, to:

My joy . . . My love . . . My peace . . . All power is given to me . . .

If we take any one of these and are simply open to them in our time of prayer we shall be opening ourselves to those attributes of God being freed to work in us and through us. This is not in any sense to hypnotise ourselves into having (or thinking we are having) lovely feelings of peace or joy or whatever. It is more a matter of being open to God in order that he can enable us to become peaceful, or joyful or loving people in the world. What Jesus speaks of as *his* peace or joy or wisdom become *my* peace or *my* joy. This is the essence of the method of prayer taught by the Fellowship of Contemplative Prayer.[1]

Boredom, then, need not be a part of our experience of the Bible if we learn to use the Bible in a way appropriate to the kind of personality God has given us. The other area of worry about the Bible is how much a person can believe, a worry which can be minimised by talking about the way in which one is to interpret this particular passage, rather than how much one can believe. Again, it might be helpful to begin by trying to get the person to be more specific about just what it is that they have difficulty with; it may be something very simple, or a particular point where they might be referred to an appropriate book for a factual answer.

More frequently, though, we are dealing with anxiety or guilt. Anxiety that things in the Bible which were once accepted as literally true no longer seem so. Guilt because, perhaps, some literal-minded friends or a narrow church may be making people feel they are not 'proper' Christians because they cannot, in all intellectual integrity, accept a literal view of the Scriptures. It is all too easy for the 'professionals' to take a symbolic understanding for granted when some of their congregations have never thought of anything other than a literal interpretation. I vividly recall some years ago at Epiphanytide preaching on the journey of the Magi and making a throwaway remark about this being a story rather than history. I had thought that Christians had accepted that for years, but found that we needed several study sessions with quite a large group of concerned people in which to begin to explore different ways of reading and interpreting the Bible.

Jowett, the great nineteenth-century scholar, once wrote of the Bible: 'Read it like any other book and you will discover it is not like any other book.' If we read the Bible like any other book we shall take from it what speaks to us and we shall not worry about what does not speak to us. Above all, we shall not let anyone make us feel guilty or 'not a proper Christian' when we do this. If you ponder over, pray about and live out all the things that do speak to you, you will be a better Christian than most of us!

It might be easiest if we were able to leave the matter at that simple and sensible point of taking what speaks to us and

21

not worrying about the rest, but those who ask questions are likely to have enquiring minds and will need to see things as a whole.

Seeing things as a whole will make it clear that, as every Sunday School child knows, the Bible is not a single book but a collection of books. This may indeed be known to every Sunday School child, but it is often forgotten by adults. No one reads a thriller in the same way as a poem, or a philosophical treatise in the same way as a children's story-book. Even intelligent adults sometimes find it hard to accept that much of the Bible is best read as poetry or story. Read in this way, with imagination, it will reveal great riches and endless applications to present-day life. For example, the story of Adam and Eve is the story of all of us, how we sense a measure of separation from God which does not seem right or intended; it is a story of how, as humans, we feel respons-ible for the whole of creation in which we live, and much, much more. It is poetry and story, rather than history, but poetry and story are in their own way just as true as history and sometimes probably more so.

Most Christains will adopt this approach to parts of the earlier books of the Old Testament; it becomes more disturb-ing when they begin to wonder whether the same might be true of parts of the gospels. I am aware as I write this that for some readers there is no problem about believing the Bible as it stands; as I said in the Introduction, if God is God, then all is possible, but those who find it all easy may find it hard to understand the minds of those for whom it is not so simple. The temptation is to become impatient or to say that such people lack faith, or to make them feel guilty or that they are not 'real Christians'. Could it not be accepted that they, too, are seekers after the truth, but that they may find that simple answers to complex questions compromise their search for the truth and their integrity? Can it not be accepted that while some desperately crave answers, others find equal fulfilment and truth in continuing to ask questions?

If you or I believe in the bodily resurrection of Jesus on the first Easter Day, is it all that dreadful that another Christian who sees in Jesus and in the best bits of the Christian tradition a way of living which is better than any other they have encountered – is it all that dreadful if that person believes the resurrection to have been more an inner realisation that the power of love, supremely present in Jesus, was not overcome by death, but continued to be alive and active in the world?

When others come to talk to us it is so important to allow them their own truth; they may in time come closer to our truth, but we do far better to affirm and encourage that which they can believe. If this toleration could develop I think that in the longer term we could be moving towards a greater richness and variety in the understanding both of the Bible and of the whole Christian tradition. But when today some demand of their church simple answers to complex questions this is, I think, another example of the church following society instead of leading it.

This rigid and simplistic approach seems to echo much of what (in England at least) was happening in politics in the 1980s. Over-simplified and imposed 'solutions' to complex questions. But the political world is changing and once again becoming more open. If the church really does follow society then we may begin to move back to a greater openness and toleration in the church as well. It is therefore to be hoped that the rigidity over the Bible fashionable today in some quarters will soften.

So when people come with worries about the Bible I think we may best help them by inviting them to treasure whatever speaks to them now, to expect that the wisdom of the past will, as they go on, provide new riches for the future, but above all, to recognise that all truth is not literal: the best truth may be poetic and symbolic. Taken as symbolic, a great deal of the hitherto unacceptable in the Bible becomes acceptable.

Is it not most helpful to encourage questioners to be realistic and down-to-earth and not to be afraid to question the Bible? I have listened again and again to people trying to 'explain', for example, some of the hairier passages of St Paul, trying to explain that Paul 'really' meant something different, as if life depended somehow on Paul, or whoever, being 'right'. Is it not healthier to believe that Paul, great person though he was, was sometimes *wrong* and that this particular bit of the Bible is *wrong*, too? . . . And if we believe Paul (or whoever) was wrong, to be able to say so openly and without guilt? It is still equally open to those who wish to justify Paul (or whoever) to do so.

So we are into the question of the authority of the Bible, and the whole question of authority seems to come back again to the differences between people. For example, there are those who will defer to someone simply because that person is a headteacher, prime minister, policeman, judge or bishop: they are authority figures. There are others who will require that authority figure to prove to us that they are trustworthy and worthy of our respect: I cannot respect a person just because he (why not 'she'?!) is a bishop. But if that person shows himself or herself to be consistently fair and just, compassionate, open and honest, then I am prepared to give them my provisional allegiance and on particular occasions the benefit of the doubt. I believe this is an honest and adult approach to authority. It does not mean that on other occasions I shall not feel entitled to challenge that authority, 'Bishop, much as I respect you, on this occasion I believe you are wrong!'

Is there not some kind of a parallel here with the way in which different people interpret the Bible? Some will say that because the church, bishops, councils of the church and so forth have declared this or that to be true they are prepared to follow that authority. This will give them security, it will save them from having to ask lots of questions, it will give a framework within which to feel free.

For others this will be experienced as an imprisonment and an assault on their integrity and their need to question and discover for themselves. Just as with worldly authority, the Bible for them will have to prove itself. If the Bible has been experienced to be consistently fair and just, compassionate, open and honest then they will be prepared to give it their provisional allegiance, and on particular occasions the benefit of the doubt. Likewise, on other occasions they will feel entitled to challenge that authority: 'Bible, much as I respect you, on this occasion I believe you are wrong!'

In thirty years of foot-slogging as a parish priest I have come to realise that there is a great gulf of incomprehension between these two kinds of people and their approach to authority of all kinds. All I am trying to do here is to ask those who find authority 'easy', to accept that the good Lord did not create all the family thus, and to try to reassure those who find themselves questioning that they can do so without guilt and without thinking that they are not 'proper Christians'.

Let that great poet, John Donne, one-time Dean of St Paul's, have the last word:

> On a huge hill,
> Cragged, and steep, Truth stands, and hee that will
> Reach her, about must, and about must goe.[2]

References

1. Peter Dodson, *Contemplating the Word* (SPCK 1987)
2. Satyre III

Why do I find it difficult to think of God as a 'person'?

When confronted by this question I again think it's import-ant to ascertain where the question may be coming from.

For some it could be a worry about a sense of loneliness, a sense of the absence rather than the presence of God, of being unloved or uncared for. If this is so, then there might be some useful discussion about where this person does find support and reassurance – what are their resources? Where are their friendships?

So often people seem to want to look for God in an other-wordly context instead of in the here and now. I believe that God works primarily through *people*, that every relationship is potentially a holy encounter, and that if our eyes and ears are open we shall become aware of a great depth and a deeper reality behind every meeting. It may not be possible for this person to envisage a personal God, but perhaps they might be helped to think of a God whose reality is mediated through the personal. I think that most of the time we undervalue our relationships with people, and I would include all those brief or casual encounters with people which we have. C.S. Lewis once observed that next to the Eucharist our neighbour was the most holy thing we should ever encounter.

Can we therefore not be more open to the wonder of each encounter, because every encounter is an opportunity for the expression of life and love? Could we not leave each meeting, however brief, with a sense of something good having happened? So for such a questioner it might be helpful to think primarily about God as mediated through other people, and supremely in Jesus, and not to worry too much about God as a person.

On the other hand, the issue may have been raised because of an intellectual inability to believe that in the immensity of creation over billions of years there could be a gigantic Divine Ear which could listen carefully to countless millions of petitions and respond to each in an appropriate manner.

It may have been possible to think of that immense Divine Ear in the days when the world was conceived of as a limited number of small nations around the Mediterranean. The Greek, Roman and other gods and goddesses were personalised as oversize human beings who listened to human petitions and responded to them in what was frequently an arbitrary way. I think that most Christians over the centuries have been content to think of God as a somewhat larger than human person – not necessarily as crude as the old man with a beard in the sky, but nevertheless as one who listens individually to their requests, waits for their thanks, and most certainly expects them to confess their sins.

It worries me that many Christians seem able to shut out from their minds the immensity of creation when they pray or otherwise think of God. It seems perfectly valid to wonder how the risen Jesus can personally listen to everything that is directed to him. Some different idea of the cosmic Christ seems to be called for, which we shall look at elsewhere.

Consider the facts. A recent newspaper article pointed out that some 15 per cent of stars have planetary systems associated with them. That adds up to 15,000,000,000 planetary systems for our galaxy alone. There are, in addition, billions of other galaxies. These are the kinds of facts which Christians so often shut their eyes to, so I think that it is helpful to discuss the difference between God as *a person* and God as *personal*. To think of God as *a person* is inevitably limiting and in the last resort comes down to a more sophisticated version of that old man in the sky with a beard. To think of God as *personal* is not to impose such limits, but to believe that the being of God

27

includes those characteristics which we ascribe to persons.

If we hold on to the idea of an intelligent creator behind all that is, a creator who continues to influence that creation, I find it hard to believe that that creator could in any way be less than personal. The problem is one of scale: perhaps the problem is our problem rather than God's problem. Our own minds are so limited, that we cannot even understand the complexity of the human brain. Within the brain of each person are thousands of circuits all interrelating with each other in harmony and unity. Is it not possible to conceive of a God whose being involves a far greater complexity which nevertheless has a unity and a similar interrelatedness where each and every tiny part matters?

Maybe we need to come back to where we started in this chapter – to recognise the absolute value of the personal in our lives, and to begin to realise that it is in the sacredness of *all* personal relationships that we can encounter something of the personship of God. Maybe you or I cannot conceive of the creator of the immensity of time and space having a personal relationship with every living creature. But that may be our inability rather than *God*'s inability.

Could we not instead think of a universe shot though with the presence of God in all people and in all things? We could then encounter through other people or things or situations, something of the wonder of God. Without trying to put any-one on a pedestal we could begin to see the glory of God, the caringness of God, expressed in and through our fellow human beings.

Many of us belong to large organisations, of which the church is one; in which no one can know everyone else, least of all the person at the top. But that would not prevent a person 'at the top' showing a care and concern for everyone in their immediate orbit, which would spread itself outwards through the organisation so that persons and personal concern become very important, reflecting the personal nature of the one in charge of the whole venture?

Could something like this be a way in which we could hold on to the validity of the idea of a personal God? You and I encounter God in the here and now, in the reality of every-day life. Every encounter and every situation is rich in pos-sibilities for actually embodying and incarnating something of the personal concern of God through ourselves.

Finally, we might enquire of the questioner whether, as they look back through life, they can see that in some strange way they have been 'held' and supported along a path which was probably better than the one they themselves might have initially wanted. I may not be very clear about the route ahead, but I'm quite clear when I look back that somehow a personal route has been indicated to me thus far in my life. I'm also very clear that prayer is frequently answered in surprising ways, and that life is littered with apparent coinci-dences which I prefer to call God-incidences.

If I want to see as clearly as I can what God is like, there is the person of Jesus to look to, who was, as Bishop John Robinson once observed, 'a window into God at work'. That is a great help. It does not, however, take away the call to look beyond to the Creator. Jesus was constantly pointing not to himself, but away from himself to the Father.

So that perhaps the barrier to belief is not so much the concept of a personal God, but rather those lingering notions of God as a person which are indeed hard to square with the immensity of creation. For my own part I continue to believe that I can still direct my aspirations, hopes and fears towards . . . who? . . . what? . . . I do not know . . . but for me there *is* a source, a direction and a destination.

Reference

1. James Hemming, *The Guardian*, November 1990

Why does the Jesus of the gospels seem so different from the Jesus of the creeds?

Imagine you have written a letter to a group of friends which you hope might possibly help them in their everyday journey to and with God. Then imagine that even within your lifetime that letter became more or less public property. People copied it and sent it to churches and communities far and wide for them to study. Then think how alarmed you would be, as the centuries went by, to find your letter being taken as a standard for what everyone else was expected to believe, and that in the hothouse of university scholarship every word was analysed and explored to find out what had influenced you in writing it.

By this time you would be finding it hard even to understand what they are talking about. Indeed, by now you might well be turning in your grave, for what was true for you at a particular time has become not only fossilised, but ever greater structures of belief have been erected upon it which others have sometimes been required to accept as true.

While you yourself were writing from your own experience, others have analysed and systematised that experience irrespective of whether or not it has also been *their* experience. If you understood what they were talking about you might wish to protest that as time had gone by your own experience and interpretation had modified or developed away from what you wrote in your letter. But you cannot make such a protest because by now you have left this world for another one.

At this point we need to come back to the third of the three kinds of theology outlined in the Introduction – experiential theology. How important is our own experience of life and our own interpretation of it? Is our own experience the bottom line for our beliefs? Is genuine belief something about a kind of integrity towards that experience? Or do we find ourselves forced by outside pressures to conformity within the church: to have to say with Galileo that the earth does not move when in our heart of hearts we know it *does* move? Are we afraid of influences in the church which may try to persuade us that unless we affirm some particular form of belief we shall be accused of not being proper Christians?

The question we are addressing is one that has been asked by Christians at every stage in the 2,000 years of Christian history: the visible church and the complex doctrines it teaches seem light years away from the village teacher roaming the lanes and byways telling people of the kingdom of God. Again and again Christians have despaired of the complexity of theology and even more of the sometimes almost demonic structures of authority in the church, and have tried to go back to what they believe Jesus himself might have said and done.

It reminds me of a joke current a few years ago. 'Jesus said to them, "Who do you say that I am?" They replied, "You are the eschatological manifestation of the ground of our being; the kerygma of which we find the ultimate meaning in our interpersonal relationships." And Jesus said, "What?" '

That is not to say that we are not called to have an intelligent faith, for the theme of this book is 'the truth shall make you free'. But it is that word 'truth' which is important; truth is to do with integrity. So if a doctrine of the church does not square with our experience of life, with our understanding of the truth, then I believe that we are entitled to let it be for the present and we should not attempt to force ourselves to say we subscribe to it. It may well be that in the fulness of time our experience of life may eventually reveal that doctrine to be valid and valuable for us.

When the kind of question at the beginning of this chapter is addressed to us, our response will depend very much on the extent of the questioner's knowledge of the Bible and of theology (and indeed of our own!). We should also want to explore with them which particular developments in belief they felt were moving away from the Jesus of the gospels. As we have already seen, the gospels were written by particular people from a particular background and at a particular point in time. To ask people to be specific rather than general is always helpful. Is it the weight of trinitarian theology which they find hard? Doctrines of incarnation or atonement? Just where is the real gap between proclaimed Christian doctrine, their own experience of life and the Jesus of the gospels (and by implication, of the epistles)?

Worries about the person of Jesus have almost always centred on the humanity and/or the divinity of Jesus. It is probably true to say that every Christian who has ever lived has placed a greater emphasis on either the humanity or the divinity. Mainline theology has insisted on an equal emphasis on each.

We know that whatever romantic ideas we might have about getting back to a simple primitive Christian faith, the truth is that even the earliest Christians did not have a single, simple, agreed understanding of Jesus. It was far more varied than we have sometimes been led to believe. What we know of the branches of Christianity that were later denounced as heretical we know largely from orthodox fulminations against them: few of the original writings survive. Imagine the view one might have 2,000 years hence of the racial situation in England in the 1960s and 1970s if only the speeches of Enoch Powell were to survive. People's understanding of Jesus was coloured, inevitably, by current beliefs of the day which provided a context, just as our own understanding will be coloured by our own context. There remain many questions about Jesus which the four gospels do little to resolve.[1]

Therefore I believe that each of us has to discover how the life of Jesus is true to our own experience of life. I can tell my story which is true for me. I do not wish to impose my story on you, but should any of my story resonate for you then it is there for you to appropriate. Likewise you can tell your story, but it is not for you to impose it on me. Still less is it for you to tell me that I am not really a Christian, let alone for you to excommunicate me or have me burned at the stake or tortured by the Inquisition. On the other hand your story may cast further light on my own story and I may wish to take some of it on board.

Each of us has to find our own way. As the Buddhist tradition expresses it, 'Even Buddhas only point the way', or as Christianity puts it, 'Work out your own salvation in fear and trembling'.[2]

So I shall listen to your story, I shall listen to your beliefs and to your doubts, without attempting to nail you as a heretic or an unbeliever, because you are granting me the great privilege of sharing your deepest experience with me. I am sure that many people never share with anyone else their deepest beliefs, the beliefs by which they really live, because they are afraid of being ridiculed or thought to be heretical or not 'proper Christians'.

The longer I live, the less I think I understand the classical formulations of christology, incarnation, atonement and salvation. With the passing of the years the words become less meaningful rather than more meaningful for me, but I do not wish to diminish in any way their importance and value for others. I also realise that we know very little for certain of the historical Jesus whose story is told from the experience of some but not all sectors of the early church. But I do know that for me, that figure of Jesus, teaching fearlessly, and confidently, of a state where God's will is done, where love reigns supreme, continues to haunt me across the decades as no other figure haunts me. Wherever Jesus was, I believe that there was made present a tiny foretaste of that which he believed would ultimately come in its fulness for all creation.

I also believe that in the totally unselfish giving of Jesus, which culminated in the events of Good Friday there came a new fulness of life which we call resurrection. The Good Friday/Easter experience is not confined to three days in history, but is lived out daily by millions of people, both Christians and others, who find a fuller quality of life in each tiny death to selfishness. The cross symbolises the need to die to our selfishness before we can find a new and fuller kind of life.

As far as all the discussion of the humanity and divinity of Jesus is concerned I am content today to say that it is *in* the very humanity of Jesus that lies the divinity. Insofar as you or I are *truly* human as Jesus was, that divinity continues to be expressed in a lesser way in the world. The divinity lies *in* Jesus being fully human, fully what he truly *was*. God is sometimes defined as pure Being, the One who truly and fully *is*. Jesus, as far as we can understand, was true to his own Being. He had an inner integrity to his deepest self and in that lay his divinity. We, too, are called to *be*, to *be* fully and completely human, fully ourselves as Jesus was fully himself, and thereby to continue to make visible something of the reality of God.

This way of loving and self-giving in which we gradually become the true and whole people God has created us to be, is the way to a fuller life, and it is something that all can experience and test out for themselves, whether or not they actually name themselves as Christians. What we see in Jesus is a way of life which is true for all humanity, and which if *followed* by all humanity would bring about the inauguration of the kingdom of God. If others wish to embroider this, that is *their* story and it may be *my* story one day in the future, or it may not, but I believe this simple understanding to be not only sufficient for me at the moment, but also true to the little that we can say without contradiction about Jesus. I do not believe that others should be pressurised by the church to attempt to affirm anything which does not yet ring true for them.

References

1. John Bowden, *Jesus, the Unanswered Questions* (SCM Press 1988) is a valuable resource.
2. Phil 2.12 (AV)

In what sense could Jesus have 'died for my sins'?

This question is closely related to the last one and it is one which people bring to me quite frequently, either openly like this, or in a more veiled form. It comes from laity and clergy alike, the latter being increasingly concerned over what they see as a 'hardening' of attitudes in the church which they feel is moving towards branding liberal Christians as either heretics or non-believers.

I have found that a good starting point is to strike a positive note and ask whether the questioner considers himself or herself to be a Christian. The answer will usually be 'yes'. Whatever others may think of them, such questioners usually consider themselves to be Christians.

I believe this needs underlining and affirming in order to build up a sometimes battered confidence. Others may have attacked that person as 'not really being a Christian'. Clergy may be under attack from their own lay people for not being sufficiently traditional or literal, which to a sensitive person can be acutely hurtful and undermining when they are simply trying to be true to their own conscience and continuing to work on their belief rather than allow it to go dead and fossilise. It would be even more painful to them to attempt to affirm something they themselves could not accept.

If our questioner is likely to affirm that she or he considers herself or himself to be a Christian we should also be likely to find agreement that Good Friday is a factual event, attested near the time by secular historians. What is at stake is the meaning of Good Friday, not its history.

Those who have difficulties with traditional formulations

of Christianity usually home down somewhere in the area of wondering how a death 2,000 years ago can make any difference to our own situation today, or how our sins could have the retrospective result of causing a death 2,000 years ago. Others have difficulty in comprehending the kind of God who could demand some kind of 'payment' for sins by punishing someone else instead, let alone the idea of the devil being allowed to demand some recompense before letting us off. And if there really was some kind of cosmic 'victory over sin', we see little evidence that human nature, even among practising Christians, is qualitatively different because of it. Many people have poked fun at Jehovah's Witnesses, who when the end of the world did not happen as predicted, asserted that the end of the world had indeed happened but that it had taken place 'spiritually'. Some may well find it hard to avoid feeling that the 'victory over sin and death' of Easter is in a somewhat similar category.

The concept of God implied in many of these approaches appears to an increasing number of Christians to be bizarre and crude in the extreme, especially when compared to Jesus' own story of the father in the parable of the prodigal son, who required neither death nor sacrifice in order to forgive. They feel that even fallen humans seem to behave rather better than the God who wants payment, or requires someone to die as a 'substitute'. And they are not helped by the church continuing to use hymns and prayers which reflect these ideas (e.g. 'There was no other good enough to pay the price of sin . . .').

It is significant and encouraging that the church as a whole has never attempted to impose any single way of understanding what happened on Good Friday. The most positive approach, it seems to me, is therefore to encourage people to articulate what they themselves think Good Friday was about without feeling the need to keep to any of the traditional paths. An ounce of honest thought-out and prayed-out belief is worth a ton of imposed interpretation against which the intellect and the integrity rebel.

When considering this question, possible starting points for discussion, thought and prayer might run along some of the following general lines.

(1) Good Friday is a fact, just as awful happenings in the world today are facts. There can be no running away from them and the Christian faith has never attempted to run away from facing up to evil and suffering. To fail to face unpleasant facts leads nowhere; to face them squarely enables realistic ways of enduring or overcoming them to be considered.

(2) According to the gospels Jesus was a totally free and authentic person. It was his tormentors who reacted consistently from fear or anger, hatred or jealousy and who thus were not free. In being totally himself, totally free to act rightly Jesus revealed his divine nature. To the extent that others are free and truly themselves, they too can reveal something of the divine nature.

But those who are 'unfree' will hate the free just as much today as they did 2,000 years ago. How often have free Christians been persecuted by unfree, compromised politicians, churchmen and others for speaking the unpalatable truth? What happened to Jesus is a salutary warning about what may happen to us if we live freely and authentically. But Easter shows us that the unfree and compromised have only a limited hold over the free and authentic.

(3) Hatred, malice and all uncharitableness cause hurt and harm to other people, but they also hurt and harm the perpetrators themselves who are ultimately diminished by the wrong that they do or say. We can all too easily forget that every action has cosmic consequences. The statement that a sneeze on the earth will have repercussions on the farthest galaxy is no mere conceit but a fact. Or, as a Christian might

express it, harm done on earth harms God as well as other people.

Good Friday shows me the hurt that human evil inflicts on God. Although the cross happened only once in time, wherever there is human awfulness, there, surely, is hurt in the heart of a loving God. So the cross remains for all time a symbol of the hurt we cause God, and in its horror it contains a power to restrain us.

(4) It is often pointed out that the helplessness of the infant Jesus and the helplessness of every child can bring out qualities of love and compassion in the most unlikely people. But helplessness and weakness can also bring out the worst, as in Matthew's story of the massacre of the innocents. So, too, with Good Friday which brought out compassion and goodness at the time and has continued to do so. The martyrdoms, the Good Fridays, of our own century have surely called forth matching acts of heroism and self-giving in countless others. One Good Friday seems to give others the courage to live boldly.

These are the seeds of some of the ideas which I have found helpful over the years. Those who ask us questions will have their own ideas which we may be able to help them develop and which we can use to encourage them. But above all, the way forward for all of us will lie in pondering and praying around those central happenings of Good Friday and Easter, for in the end I believe that it is God who will grant us insight as a gift.

Who knows what illuminating and exciting insights into the crucifixion and resurrection have been lost, perhaps for ever, because the ordinary person who was given those insights was worried about their value, or hesitated to express them because they were new. Perhaps they were clobbered by the 'experts' because their ideas did not fit in with a more approved traditional doctrine?

I should want to say to the questioner, 'Is that insight into God true to your experience?', and if it is, to continue to test it against ongoing experience; and also, choosing open and loving people who will not kill your insight at birth, to invite those others to consider whether your insight might also be true to their experience.

I am not trying to suggest or imply that the traditional doctrines of the atonement no longer have any validity. I am simply trying to suggest that if people have difficulty with them they do not necessarily need to consider themselves unbelievers. And nobody should do anything to make them feel rejected or guilty or not 'really Christian'.

Part Two

QUESTIONS
ABOUT PRAYER

Is anybody there?

I was first confronted with a form of this question nearly thirty years ago when I was a very junior priest in my first curacy. It was addressed to me by an intelligent young confirmation candidate. I haven't the remotest recollection as to how I responded, but I'm sure my reply was totally useless.

At the time I had not been a Christian for all that long. I had been a cheerful agnostic for ten years and had been dragged reluctantly back into 'the church thing' after a major religious experience, after which the reality of God had remained for me almost overwhelming. I felt like an expanse of dry desert into which refreshing water had flooded, bringing dead things to life and blossom. God was very close and very real, so that in attempting to respond to that young person I'm sure I must have made some bland affirmation of my own belief. Maybe I tried to reassure her. It certainly would not have occurred to me to go more deeply into her question and ask what she understood by God or what things in life were the most important for her. But the golden rule seems to me now to be never to try to respond to a complex question without exploring it in much more detail and without asking what lies behind the question or finding out whether there are misunderstandings.

It was only later that I came to realise that the questioner's experience (or absence of experience) was something which most believers encounter at some stage or another, and in some cases it remains for long periods of time. Thirty years later the people I worry about are not those with a sense of blankness, but those who never seem to have had this sense of 'there's nothing there', and who still live in apparent total certainty.

43

Given the way the question is phrased, it seems that it comes typically from people who consider themselves Christians because they seem to be praying regularly. It might be helpful to ask them about their image of God (or they may well have quite a number of images of God). For some, their picture of God will essentially be that of Jesus himself, so that prayer for them will be essentially what I would call without any implication of condescension, 'talking to Jesus'. If so, how do they see him? As a contemporary figure or as a historical figure? In visual terms? Or simply as a felt presence alongside them?

If that picture of Jesus is no longer helpful to them it may mean that the time has come for them to think more in terms of the reality of Christ in other people, and thus to expand and extend their understanding of him. To be able to take this step of being open to and aware of Christ in others may be of enormous importance in deepening their faith.

On the other hand, to ask someone about their image (or images) of God may produce a somewhat guilty response because they are unable to picture or sense the person of Jesus present with them. It may be hard for Christians who are primarily 'Jesus-centred' to take this on board. Not all Christians find they pray most naturally to the person of Jesus, and if they are surrounded by Christians who *do* pray in this way, they may feel that they are somehow not 'proper' Christians, or that they have missed some essential experience.

They need not worry, for some Christians pray more readily to God as Creator, or to God as the indwelling Holy Spirit and when they pray they find it helpful to think of the glory of God in creation, or the reality of the Holy Spirit dwelling deep within them. They should not worry if at present the person of Jesus seems remote. Others find it helpful to see reflections of Jesus in the great Christians we call saints: if the reality of Jesus at times seems distant, the saints may be a way towards the vision, though we need to remember that each saint will reflect only a tiny glimmer of the glory of the cosmic Christ.

To invite people to consider their image of God may help them to understand why there may sometimes seem to be 'nothing there'. It may be that they are being called to move on to another kind of prayer or they may have been trying to think of God in a way that is unhelpful to the kind of person they are.

Again, there are many male images of God around, 'Father' being the most common. But how about the person who has had only a very bad experience of human fathering? For them it may be very hard to address a God who is envisaged in this way, so that nurturing, caring, mothering images of God may be a more helpful way into prayer. Someone once told me that their image of God was of someone with very penetrating eyes. It turned out that this person's father had bullied him and rubbished everything he did. So much so that there was a great deal of guilt around, along with a strong drive to overwork and a sense of never being able to please. This had transferred itself on to God, who for them could never be pleased however much they worked themselves to a standstill.

It may, then, be helpful to explore the appropriateness or otherwise of people's images of God. If they are inappropriate images there will be little sense of any meaningful relationship with God.

I think what most frequently happens is that people have had good experiences in the past, maybe in personal prayer, maybe in church services, maybe at other times, but they now find they no longer have that kind of experience. God for them has become identified with a particular kind of experience, and if that kind of experience has gone, God, too, seems to have gone, and this can be very upsetting. Yet the way forward is not the way back! It never is. If I am only looking for my friend coming from one direction I shall miss him if he approaches from the opposite direction. The important thing is not to think of God in any particular way, but to be open at all times to a sense of wonder and awe, a sense of joy or love or beauty. Later on in this book we shall look at finding God in painful situations, but for the moment let's stay with the positive ones. Some Christians seem only to be able to think of encountering God when they are praying and yet the whole world is shot through with the glory of God! We go through most of our lives unaware, with our eyes and ears shut as if we were on automatic pilot. Try taking a day – or just a few hours – in which you do not specifically set out to pray, but do just what you *want* to do, however totally secular this may seem. Take your time over whatever it is, try to be aware of everything around you, to be aware of your own feelings, thoughts and sensations and I should be surprised if you do not emerge with a sense of your life having been enhanced and that you have been in touch with something greater than yourself. You may not even want to speak of God but simply to treasure the experience. We are so inclined to confine God to our prayer-time that we may cease to be aware of the glory around us and within us.

What I call 'retrospective awareness' is also helpful to many people. In the bustle of everyday life, most of us dash from one activity to another without giving ourselves time to reflect on where God might be in a situation. So it is all the more important to sit down quietly at some stage each day to reflect on the twenty-four hours we have just lived, to look at what we did and whom we met, at what we heard and experienced, and to go on asking, 'Where was God in that?'

Most of the time, sadly, we have been set on that automatic pilot, half-asleep, but there will have been enough situations where we were more aware – situations in which we can now realise that God was giving or challenging or asking. We may not be able to picture God, but we may be able to discern his *activity* around us and in us. As I might have said to my young confirmation candidate, you cannot see the wind, but you can see its effects.

At the end of the day, though, all images and pictures of God are inadequate, and a sense that there is no one or nothing there may simply be a sign that our current ideas or images of God are now inadequate to our needs. There is a lovely prayer by George Appleton, which I have already quoted in my previous book, which needs re-quoting here. He called his prayer 'Images':

Christ, my Lord, again and again I have said with Mary Magdalene, 'They have taken away my Lord and I know not where they have laid him.'
I have been desolate and alone.
And you have found me again, and I know that what has died is not you, my Lord, but only my idea of you, the image which I have made to preserve what I have found, and to be my security. I shall make another image, Lord, better than the last. That, too, must go, and all successive images, until I come to the blessed vision of yourself, O Christ, my Lord.

It is helpful to remember the essential paradox of a God who is infinitely close, knowable and accessible to us and yet at the same time a God who is infinitely greater than we can even begin to conceive, who is in a sense 'unknowable' or 'incomprehensible'.

We can readily know the energies of a God as manifested in the natural world, in people, in the course of history, but God in his essence is unknowable. In prayer we frequently break through the energies of God in the search for the essence of God and find ourselves apparently confronted with nothing. If the questioner is referring to this experience it can at first be frightening. She or he may need helping to come back to the energies of God for reassurance, at least until it becomes 'all right' to live with that disorienting sense of there being 'nothing there'. In fact it's all right to be there and it is usually a healthy, if uncomfortable place to be.

Professor Maurice Wiles expresses the point about the energy and essence of God like this:

> The point [in Eastern Orthodox Christianity] of ultimate paradox is the distinction of the divine essence and the divine energies. Both are uncreated, both are fully divine; there is a distinction but not a division between them; they are not two parts of God, but two modes of his existence, in the one of which he is utterly unknowable, in the other of which he is infinitely giveable to man. 'The divine nature', says Lossky, 'must be called at the same time incommunicable and in a sense communicable; we attain participation in the nature of God and yet he remains totally inaccessible. We must preserve both things at once and must preserve the antinomy as the criterion of piety.[1]

I have a suspicion that it is often at those times when God seems most unreal to us in prayer, when we really do wonder whether there is anybody or anything there at all, that we can be most penetratingly aware of the glory of God 'out there' in the world and in people. It is as if in his goodness God is compensating us for one apparent loss with an even bigger gift than usual elsewhere.

Reference

1. Maurice Wiles, *The Re-making of Christian Doctrine* (SCM Press 1974) pp.109–10

Is prayer really 'talking to Jesus'?

I think we need to be critical of what goes on in our churches – constructively critical – because an increasing number of Christians seem to have a spirituality which is totally and exclusively centred upon Jesus. It is important to remember that Jesus was constantly pointing away from himself towards the Father, the Creator. Our questioner may well want to follow that guidance and centre prayer primarily on God as Creator, thereby entering into the unfathomable mystery of God. Alternatively, people may find that their prayer moves more naturally inwards and that they are centring more on the reality of the Spirit of God within them.

It often calls for quite a lot of courage to withstand group pressure and continue to affirm what is true for us in the face of criticism. I am acutely aware of having been accused many times in my life of not being a real Christian, and I know how much this hurts. It assaults one's integrity and attempts to force one into a single narrow mould as well as attempting to rubbish one's deeply held beliefs, the beliefs by which, with all one's failings, one tries to live.

It is, is it not, a matter of tolerance. 'Talking to Jesus' in one form or another is indeed the heart of prayer for millions of Christians. There are highly regarded ways of praying which are essentially 'talking to Jesus' even in those parts of the church where this is not really the norm. The Jesus prayer of the Orthodox Church is a 'talking to Jesus' prayer: the well-known exercise of 'the empty chair' is just as much 'talking to Jesus'. We imagine that there is an empty chair beside us. It may indeed be helpful to put a real empty chair there, and we imagine Jesus sitting there. We begin a conversation, making sure that it is not one-sided.

But this kind of prayer does not suit everyone. If it does not help the person we are talking to we shall want to explore what kinds of prayer *are* meaningful for this person and we shall probably need to reassure them that their path is perfectly all right.

We shall, however, want to help them to articulate in a little more detail just what is worrying them. For some it may be simply that they find other ways of praying than 'talking to Jesus' lead to a greater awareness of God. Their worry may be exacerbated in some circles by group pressures to understand prayer simply as 'talking to Jesus'. But most frequently there will be some kind of intellectual reservation.

We shall probably find that the intellectual reservation is to do with just *how* they understand Jesus. For some Christians it is perfectly natural to imagine the risen, ascended Lord alongside them as a continuing human person with whom they can converse. To other Christians this will seem rather like a child going through a phase of having an imaginary 'friend' with whom they have imaginary conversations. (I realise that even to suggest this will offend many, but we are trying to face up to how other people may feel.) Such a reaction does not of course invalidate this way of praying. For some Christians, as they consider the unimaginable extent of the universe, existing back in time and into the future for countless aeons, it is impossible to imagine a single human figure giving attention to each individual. They can still realise that we all matter, that we are all loved but the idea of a single person split into billions of listening ears defies their belief.

If people come to talk to us about this they may well be feeling vaguely guilty or that they no longer belong. It is therefore important to try to help them towards some under-

standing of Jesus which will make sense to them. Most probably they already do have such an understanding and need
only to be reassured that it is all right to be where they are.
Also, if we are genuinely seeking the truth, our understanding of God and of Jesus will go on developing all through our
lives.

I find, as I talk to other people, that they seldom have
problems with thinking about the person of Jesus 2,000 years
ago. No problems with the person who gathered friends
around him, women and men, and who moved them to become channels of the love of God, to begin to bring about the
kingdom of God, where God's will would be done on earth
as it was in heaven. But that human figure of Jesus is no
longer for them the tangible, physical reality he was for his
friends 2,000 years ago. They might, though, be able to
understand Jesus in the way outlined in Chapter 5; namely
that the divinity of Jesus lay in his freedom and authenticity,
rather than in some complex merging of two forms of being,
human and divine, as is traditionally taught. To be fully
human is to express the divinity appropriate to the human
being, just as to be a tree in all its glory is to express the glory
of God appropriate to that tree.

It would therefore follow that to the extent that other
human beings have lived free and authentic lives they, too, in
a humbler way have also expressed just a little of the glory,
the divinity of God. In other words, Christ continues to be
expressed daily in our world of today, through you and me.
It is essentially, therefore, in our neighbour that we should
seek to discover the living, risen Christ.

This, I find, is what many Christians who come to talk to
me believe, and in my view it is no diminishment of Jesus of
Nazareth, but a joyful and exciting realisation of the cosmic
Christ in our own world of today. This is not in any sense to
undermine or devalue those who think of prayer primarily as

'talking to Jesus', although they, too, might find it helpful to consider how far God as Creator and God as indwelling Holy Spirit is also a part of their prayer. It is, rather, to give encouragement to those who find Christ primarily in the everyday world of the present moment rather than in an exercise of the imagination which envisages an invisible Christ.

Those who take a more traditional view may respond by saying that 'if the resurrection was real, and Jesus appeared to his disciples he must surely "be" somewhere now. And if he is divine, then surely he may well be "there" listening to all the prayers and thoughts being offered.'

I am not trying to deny the beliefs of anyone. All I am trying to do here is to affirm that we all need the confidence to live with such truths as we have been given and which we are at the moment able to receive. Much of what we call spiritual direction is a matter of reasuring those who fear they may be on the wrong path, or who have been battered by those who believe that they and only they are right. There are, of course, dangerously wrong paths, and discernment is important, which is why it is wise for all Christians to be able to talk from time to time to another Christian.

So then, pray as you can and not as other people may tell you that you should!

What's wrong with yoga?

This may seem to most readers a very naive question: surely there are more important ones? Many Christians have gained from some of the insights of yoga and there is a considerable literature on Christian yoga.[1] However, I have included this question because it may help to illuminate an important general point. I have taken yoga as but one example of a whole range of activities and insights which some Christians regard as if they were the invention of the devil. There is at stake here a principle of much wider application than the value or danger of yoga. The criticism – insofar as it is clearly articulated – seems to be that there could be some imbibing of something evil because yoga has its origin in a different culture.

I think I would first want to discover what kind of yoga the questioner has found helpful. It will probably be a form of Hatha yoga as taught on thousands of adult education courses (and in church halls!) all over the country. It is generally a matter of simple breathing and relaxation exercises and held bodily positions which improve awareness, agility and health.

If one were to offer these to people simply as keep fit exercises without using the word 'yoga' my guess is that no one would complain and indeed I recall from my far-off schooldays having done quite a bit of what might be called yoga during 'gym' lessons. Can it really be that if we call an activity 'yoga' it is sinful and harmful but if we don't call it yoga it's all right? Those who object to yoga might reasonably question whether the exercises or relaxation had anything to do with prayer, but that is another issue. In the unlikely event of the yoga involving a belief system one would obviously wish to question more closely, but I'm concerned by those who react with an unthinking conditioned reflex to a word without first pausing to explore what it is really all about.

If our bodies are temples of the Holy Spirit then we have a responsibility to God to care for those bodies. If that care involves helping us to relax and be more open to God in prayer, it seems very questionable to deny the reality of another person's good experience without closer knowledge. Indeed, it seems to me tantamount to calling good evil, and Jesus had something very fierce to say about that.[2] At the very least one is calling the other person stupid or deluded.

If we discover that our questioner is simply talking about exercises, postures and breathing (as will very probably be the case), a bit of simple common sense and a sense of humour would probably encourage them to continue. But is that enough? Should we not invite a counter-challenge to the criticism of yoga? Underlying the criticism are three assumptions, all of which I believe to be dangerous and life-denying.

The first we have seen as a rubbishing and denial of that which another person (indeed many persons) has found helpful and not in any way at odds with their Christian insight. Why should the objector's absence of experience entitle them to pontificate on a subject over and above one who has experienced it and benefited from it? A genuine seeking of others is being criticised as evil. It reminds one of the way the pre-Reformation church made itself look stupid over the rotation of the earth round the sun just as a later church was made to look stupid in its attempted denial of the fact of evolution.

It is probably true to say that whenever Christians have tried to argue from a literal intepretation of the Bible in the face of carefully evaluated evidence and experience they have been made to look silly. The Bible is there to be interpreted more broadly as one factor among others. God has given us our reason and our experience and therefore presumably expects us to use them!

Secondly, the criticism of yoga can imply a narrowness in understanding how God communicates with us. It is all too easy to become brainwashed into thinking that religious knowledge can only come to us through words. Anything other than words seems to be frightening to some Christians, hence the denial of movement, colour, ceremony and even musical instruments in some forms of worship. God is perceived directly and immediately through the senses, and this, with its unexpectedness and lack of control is frightening for those who are insecure. It seems far safer, they seem to feel, to confine their knowledge of God to words, because words are processed through the mind. Words can be controlled and are at least one remove from reality. Yet the more that scholars have pondered over the nature of language the less sure they have become about the degree of clarity which can be achieved by it.

The third assumption is the most frightening, and it brings before us perhaps the most challenging of all divisions of opinion among Christians. It seems to me that when anything to do with yoga is seen as dangerous the underlying assumption is that there can be no truth unless it is specifically 'Christian', that other religions have nothing to teach us, and that there can be no such thing as a dialogue with people of other faiths; only Christians have the truth.

I quite frequently hear an even more alarming undertone, which seems to be suspicious of any knowledge whatsoever unless it can be vouched for somewhere in the Bible – as if all humanity's later experience of God since the closing of the canon of the Bible counts for nothing. It seems to postulate the curious view that the world 'out there' is full of evil, or a very powerful devil. So that we have to drag everyone out of

55

the real world into a secondary artificial world, a holy huddle of Christians meeting endlessly for protection from atheists, agnostics, Hindus, Buddhists, New Agers, yoga teachers . . . and much else besides. Is it not healthier to have our eyes open for signs of God in the real world created by him, to see creation as a glorious work of God?

The alternative is a view which leads to a ghetto mentality: unless you are one of us you are totally outside. In recent years churches with a ghetto mentality have been increasing, but I believe that they will only attract the immature and guilt-laden, and that they can only keep their members by playing on the guilt levels with an authoritarian form of ministry. Their appeal is ultimately as limited as their vision of Christianity.

For the Christian, the good news is for all people. It is 'catholic' in the original sense of the word meaning 'universal'. The spirit of the Lord fills the world; God can be discovered in anybody or anything. We can learn something from people of other faiths which will illuminate and enlarge our Christian insights. Indeed, I believe that the whole Christian understanding of suffering and death, resurrection and the life-giving nature of love is something which is true not simply for paid-up Christians, but is a dynamic of human life which is true for everyone. Each world religion seems to have discovered something of it.

Today, we face situations never envisaged by the writers of the Bible, where we have few guidelines other than a belief in the life-giving nature of sacrificial love and the power of God to create and to heal.

So our questioner really has a choice between two world-systems: a world-view where only the Bible and the Christian tradition are 'safe', or a world view where God is in creation and there are many ways of coming to know that God. If people come to talk to us about this kind of thing I believe we have a duty under God to make as clear as we can the implications lying behind each of those two world-views.

References

1. See, for example, Herbert Slade, *Exploration into Contemplative Prayer* (Darton Longman and Todd 1975); J. M. Dechanet OSB, *Christian Yoga* (Search Press 1960) and *Yoga and God* (Search Press 1974)
2. Matthew 12.31–2

How can I trust God when the people I pray for go on suffering?

I make no apology for including this question although as I write it I can almost hear the cynical snort of the reader: 'So he thinks he's going to answer the problem of suffering in four pages flat'. Or the weary resignation of other readers: 'What's the point of including this since he's going to say that he's not going to *attempt* to find an answer to the problem of suffering in four pages flat'.

I include it because in one form or another this question lies beneath an enormous amount of one-to-one talking, and I doubt whether we can have progressed very far along the Christian path if we have not asked it for ourselves.

The fact that we have no wholly satisfying answer for ourselves does not dispense us from trying to be as sensitive as we can to others who may also be struggling with this question. Above all, we shall avoid giving pat answers. Each sufferer – and that means all of us – has to discover their own way of living with the question. And if we are called upon to be listeners we have a responsibility to stay alongside in the suffering. That staying alongside may indeed be all that we *can* do. And it is very much more than most people are prepared to do.

All too readily Christians shut their eyes to the pain of the world and try to pretend that everything is wonderful. At the convent where I work for a part of my time we follow a series of readings which includes a section of a psalm between the epistle and the gospel, used as a repeated response from the congregation. The responses laid down are almost entirely ones affirming the love, goodness and mercy of God.

But where then is the bewilderment before God? Where is the despair? The anger? The incomprehension? Why do liturgists remove all those anguished bits from the psalms for the Eucharist? During the Gulf War, with thousands of civilians and soldiers being killed as they fled from Kuwait, I found it very hard to praise the loving mercy and compassion of God.

I think it is important to recognise that we shall all have different attitudes at different times in our lives. At a time of acute misery or pain or depression we may hold views which we do not hold at other times. Indeed, we may desperately need to express our doubts and agony and questioning to another person before we can realise that this is not, after all, the whole story.

In much the same way I may need to be able to express anger or resentment about a person to a few trusted friends or colleagues so that when I actually meet that person I can behave normally towards them and begin to realise that my anger or resentment is not the whole story and that I was probably being unfair. My friends, though, have been very important; they will know that my anger is not the whole of me and that it can be neutralised or later put into perspective. We may all have a desperate need to express to someone else our anger or mistrust of God; and in the very expression of it, we may find when we face the world again that our anger at God was not the whole story. There have after all been times in all our lives when we have known that God *has* been trustworthy.

Depending on the situation it may or may not be helpful to invite people to explore ways in which they have understood the love and care of God at more positive times, but I am sure that it is preferable to help people express their own ideas about the love of God rather than for anyone else to attempt to impose their own viewpoint which others may have tested and found wanting, and which to hear again can only make them feel more despairing.

There are many Christians who are unable to express their anger or disappointment directly to God. It would be better all round if they could. I don't mean by this that God doesn't already know that we are angry or mistrustful or whatever, but the articulation of our feelings can help towards a resolution. It opens the channel between us and God. There is some kind of parallel here with the everyday situation in which people seem to expect us to know how they are feeling without their having told us: 'You should have known I was angry', they might say, and I want to reply, 'But why? You never told me! If you had told me you were angry we could have talked and maybe resolved it.'

Bringing matters openly to God, bringing the whole of ourselves, even the unacceptable bits, is part of growing closer to God. Again it's much the same in a human relationship. We begin by being ever so nice to each other and enjoying the things about which we agree, but that relationship will never progress beyond a superficial level until we have been brave enough to let the other person know where we disagree and to allow them to see the disagreeable bits of ourselves. 'I shall call you no longer servants . . . I call you friends', said Jesus.[1] And friends share the angry bits as well as the nice bits.

Our role may be to listen and absorb some of the negative feelings in order to help a person realise that they do not always feel this way about God. We can explore with them what are their more positive ways of understanding the pain they see around them, and help them to begin some kind of dialogue with God about it. I increasingly encourage people to write down some of these things, and when they have written down their negative feelings about God, I invite them to pause and listen to see what may be coming back and to write that down too. I am not suggesting that what comes back will necessarily be the authentic voice of God – it may be the more positive part of ourselves – but I do believe that in prayer of this kind insights and help are frequently given to us.

In encouraging others to talk, listeners may often find the views they themselves hold being threatened or challenged. It is very easy to hit back with some orthodox response ('the church teaches . . .'), but I think we need to respect the honesty of that other person's search for truth, even if it seems to be leading them into strange byways. They may, perhaps, be seeing pain and suffering as a dark or shadow side of God. The Bible, with its record of the anger or wrath of God, gives some justification for this view, whether or not at the end of the day we reject it as inadequate. People may begin to question whether the term 'God' is particularly helpful in this context of suffering and simply prefer to think of the ultimate human importance of loving and being loved.

I don't think that the listener is necessarily precluded from expressing how he or she sees the matter, especially if a view has been requested. But this is not the listener stating magisterially the teaching of the church: it is rather a sharing of views, 'It seems to me that . . .' or 'I'd see it something like this . . .' This respects the integrity of the other either to accept or reject what we say. All statements should imply a question mark at the end: 'This is so . . . is it not?'

I have long thought that we Christians all too often forget, in times of suffering, the whole question of human freedom, and put all the weight on the other side of the paradox, namely the omnipotence of God. I can blame God, we say, for this suffering, this failure to answer prayer the way I wanted it answered, because God has not used his omnipotence to put things right. This ignores the fact that we have at least a limited amount of freedom of choice in the world which must in some way affect God's own freedom. If it were not so, my own freedom would be a mirage. I believe that the cross was in part God's reminder to us that the price of freedom is a measure of handing over of power by God, a God who also shares in the suffering.

One of the great privileges of being a spiritual director is that relationships often continue over many years. Again and again I have sat alongside people in the depths of misery and doubt, feeling totally helpless and seeing no possible way out of an awful situation. But as time has gone on that person's perspective has altered, things have changed and God has become real and trustworthy again for them.

Even as I write this I see on my desk a letter which arrived only this morning from someone who after years of wretched struggling with just this question of pain, suffering and unanswered prayer, has found the reality of God once more in a far deeper way than ever before. The letter reads, 'I never thought I'd feel like this again.' No one propounded or attempted to propound 'answers' in the dark time – they would not have made sense, and with some kinds of personality would probably push a person over the edge into a total rejection of God. We can only wait on God, but we can also be ready to challenge God and to share our anguish with others who are not going to be shocked or, like Job's 'comforters', propound the 'easy' answers of orthodoxy. Each person has to come to his or her own truth about God.

Reference

1. John 15.15 (NJB)

Part Three

QUESTIONS
ABOUT BELONGING

QUESTION 10

Why do I seem to have more in common with non-Christians?

This is one version of a question which comes in various forms. Many years ago when I attended a selection conference to see whether the church was prepared to ordain me, we were all asked to discuss (under close observation, of course!) the statement, 'I find more friendship at the Pig and Whistle on Sunday evenings than I do at Evensong.'

It is all too easy to brush off that form of the question with some glib evasion like, 'Of course, that's what the Pig and Whistle is for'. It is true that we have come to Evensong to pray rather than to have a pint with our friends, but is it not reasonable after Evensong to hope for signs of friendship, however brief, which at least equals what we shall shortly find in the pub? During the early years of Christianity it was not from cynicism but in admiration that an outsider exclaimed, 'See how these Christians love each other.' That experience is a far cry from the experience of many Christians today. Repeatedly over the years I have had the traumatic experience of going to greet someone at the Peace during the Eucharist to find them turning away, head in the air.

Such a question is usually about a sense of disillusionment with the visible church. No one can be a Christian for very long without encountering it in one form of another or without also asking the same somewhat despondent question about the unfriendliness, narrowness, judgmentalism and petty-mindedness among all too many Christians. We see the arrogance of the young Christian, and the cantankerousness of the elderly Christian who appears to have shrunk rather than grown in the faith over the years. It is made harder because of the love and friendship which most of us have received from those who do not call themselves Christians.

The temptation is to try to defend the church and to make disparaging remarks about the caring agnostic. I have even heard it claimed that the agnostic's caring is really only selfish and that it would not stand up in a time of trial. I don't think this is good enough; quite apart from being untrue, it is extremely arrogant. I find it painful to read the unbelievably uncharitable letters which recur in the church press. It is also painful to try to work with lifelong Christians who live in a world of such selfishness and narrow-mindedness that most unbelievers would be shocked. I think it is a further cop-out to try to turn the question back on the questioner and to suggest that we should first look at our own faults before blaming other Christians. Of course I know the saying about motes and beams and it may indeed be the case that we are spotting tiny motes in other people while missing the beams in our own eyes, and this is something we need to be constantly aware of. But the questioner is usually talking about a sense of shock or despair that some professiong Christians or even a whole congregation should be so awful; or that a decision of a synod should be so life-denying and unloving.

I think it is far better to acknowledge the awfulness. Jesus reserved his harshest condemnation for those who thought they were good, that is for the 'church' of his day. The Old Testament prophets likewise reserve their fiercest condemnation for those who think they are the 'true' church of their day. When a good thing turns sour it is worse than a mediocre thing going sour; when religion goes wrong it is nastier than anything else. There are few things more shocking than the Inquisition or the persecution and torturing of Christians by Christians on all sides at the time of the Reformation.

Some of the Reformers, looking at the awfulness of the visible church, asked themselves the question, 'Who constitutes the true church?' They felt that the true church could hardly be the church which they could see, so perhaps the membership of 'the true church' was known only to God and might well contain many people who would not have thought of themselves as belonging to the church at all.

Such a view never found general favour, perhaps because it would have hit at the power structures of the visible church. But there is something of value there. To look at the unlovingness and narrowness of some who speak in the name of the church and to look at the saintliness (no less) of some agnostics, and then to try to justify the first group while denying the integrity of the second seems to be a case of calling evil good and good, evil.

So that when people say – as I readily acknowledge having said myself on many occasions – that they have far more in common with caring agnostics than with many Christians, I think we need to recognise just how dreadfully wrong religion can go. The heart of the caring agnostic seems to me to be a readiness to go on searching for the truth and, as we noted at the start of this book, 'the truth shall make you free.' To go on searching for the truth implies a readiness to admit that we may be wrong and have to start again. So many people who call themselves Christians seem so certain that they have the truth and that others are wrong, that they simply do not seem able to listen to other voices.

But there are countless people in the world who are honestly and genuinely seeking for the truth. They are on a journey but they have not so far found the truth within the Christian church, perhaps because of the behaviour of some Christians. In my work I hear from time to time terrible accounts of people who have been sexually abused in childhood or adolescence by Christians or even by Christian ministers. Without intensive counselling or therapy, how can they be expected to work out their journey to God within the visible Christian church?

To some Christians, a belief that they are somehow different from other people, that they are 'saved' while others are not 'saved' seems to be important. Why do they want to feel somehow special or better than others or 'chosen' while others, they believe, are not chosen? I think I want somehow to validate that ministry at the Pig and Whistle; to validate the caring of the agnostic and to say that we are all a part of the one human race created by God and loved equally by God. St Peter said, 'God has no favourites, but . . . in every nation the one who is godfearing and does what is right is acceptable to him.'[1]

The important thing doesn't seem to be whether we can affirm that we are saved or we belong to the church or that we believe in every article of faith in the Apostles' Creed. Rather, is is not more important that we are searching for the truth, refusing to call good evil or evil, good and acknowledging goodness wherever we find it, trying to live in love and peace with each other in the power which God gives us? If the visible church cannot do this it may yet have to die; but even if it dies that will not extinguish the presence of the spirit of Christ in all who are seeking the truth and trying to live in the power of love.

So if we are confronted by those who find more in common with caring agnostics than with many Christians, let's not try to defend the indefensible, but rather look for the good and the loving wherever they may be, recognising in awe and wonder that *there* God is present.

Many will disagree, but in the final analysis I am coming to believe that the important thing is to be as fully human as we can, developing all the potential God has given us. To the extent that this happens I believe we shall also discover that we are becoming Christians in the true sense of the word, sharing something of the nature of Christ, the one fully human person.

Reference

1. Acts 10.34 (NEB)

QUESTION 11

Do I have to agree with everything people say in church?

> Take my silver and my gold
> Not a mite would I withhold.

So runs the hymn, but staid members of the congregation would take fright if they were taken at their word and required to empty their pockets and make out a cheque for the whole of their bank balance. Over-the-top emotional statements need balancing with reality, and it is dishonest to expect congregations to make affirmations way beyond the point they have reached.

Particularly unfair are those occasions when people at services or prayer groups are asked unexpectedly to make some major act of dedication. There is a question of integrity here. An act of dedication or offering requires long and prayerful thought.

For many years I used to conduct retreats for the Fellowship of Contemplative Prayer. In these retreats we often used a prayer in which we offered to God 'all that we are, all that we have and all that we hope for'. One could not offer much more than that! However, this offering was tempered by the important proviso, 'as far as we are able'. That realistic proviso allowed for a progressive offering of ourselves over the years as we hopefully became more committed. 'All-or-nothing' responses seem fine at the time, but in the cold light of day there is often something dishonest about them. Turning to the light is something we need to do again and again, turning a little further each time. The Fellowship of Contemplative Prayer dedication recognised this and responded honestly to it.

In church services there will inevitably be a tension between those statements which are true for us now and those which are essentially aspirations for the future and about which we should do well to say quietly, 'as far as I am able'. It is also worth recalling that in any corporate act of worship there will be people at different stages along the Christian road and some of the statements may be for them rather than for us. Those who have responsibility for organising services need to be particularly sensitive in what they ask people to say. To offer everything to God may mean something comparatively easy for some people: for others, it would mean nothing less than living in a cardboard box and starving.

Aspirations are one thing; statements of belief are another, and these can be particularly difficult for clergy of the Anglican, Orthodox and Roman Catholic traditions who are normally required to use the agreed orders of service. I have a great fellow feeling for clergy who say that as they stand behind the altar they need to demythologise many of the things they are required to say ('instant translation' was how one priest expressed it). At the same time as being concerned about their own integrity they may also be worrying as to whether they should be doing that instant translation for their congregations. Is it fair to leave a congregation thinking that their priest believes a statement literally when in reality he accepts it symbolically or poetically? Is it not even harder for a lay person in the congregation to do this instant translation than for the clergy? The clergy will at least be likely to be saying to themselves, 'Well, for me this really means . . .' while members of the congregation may well be saying to themselves, 'I don't believe that', which isn't really very helpful.

There will of course be others for whom the literal words continue to make good sense, so there can never be a clear solution other than mutual tolerance. Good preaching and good teaching can, of course, resolve a lot of things, but one recalls that the most sacred words in our worship, 'This is my body . . . this is my blood', convey a whole range of different meanings to different traditions in the church.

There remains a pressing need for new liturgies which do not need instant internal translation and for congregations to begin to write their own prayers, hymns and liturgies which express what is true for them. I know of no better way of helping Christians to work out what they really believe than to write their own prayers and liturgies. Worship is not just words; but organists and clergy can easily choose hymns simply because they enjoy the tune, neglecting the more pressing fact that the words may be something of an affront. On the positive side, good liturgy speaks as much through movement, positioning and action as through language, and sensitive attention to ceremonial and arrangement can often convey a more acceptable meaning than some of the words.

If people come to talk to us about this I again think it helps to ask them to be specific. If they simply have a generalised disaffection with church services, we are very likely to find, on further investigation, that this has more to do with personalities than with doctrine, more to do with the new vicar or the organist than with their understanding of the Eucharist.

I realise that all this may seem a bit bland and reassuring, compared with the anxiety and lack of integrity that some priests and ministers, including myself, can feel when conducting a service. But I find it salutary to remind myself that over the years both those who talk to me and I myself have altered and hopefully grown in the faith. Ideas and visions have changed and for every statement I have doubted

71

another has been illuminated with a new and fresh meaning. So while new prayers and liturgies which express our own position are valuable, to include in services only what we can at the moment accept would deprive us of great riches and possibilities for future growth. God is a mystery and the fact that we do not understand is no reason not to go on trying to see what might lie behind the obscurities or even the parts we disagree with.

But I think that the major difficulty is that we want to take as literal that which is poetic or symbolic. Released from the literal our faith gains a new freedom.

Reference

1. See earlier reference to the Fellowship of Contemplative Prayer at the end of Chapter 2.

Why does church seem so disconnected from the rest of my life?

I think I can best begin this chapter by telling a little of my own story.

Many years ago I found myself in Japan, doing National Service in that long-forgotten campaign, the Korean war. The headquarters of British Commonwealth Forces Korea was based not in Korea, but in the former Japanese naval base of Kure, some 20 miles from Hiroshima. At that time, before going up to Oxford, I was in an agnostic phase which lasted for ten years. However, my agnostic composure had been jolted by my posting to Korea. Around me, my compatriots were receiving postings to West Germany, Singapore, even (bless 'em!) to Bermuda, while I was a sacrificial lamb about to be offered up on the Korean altar.

I panicked briefly and before going on embarkation leave went, shamefacedly, to talk as a frightened agnostic to the Army chaplain. I shall never forget his sound earthy commonsense. He took down from his bookshelf a book of statistics and showed me how, on the basis of World War II, the level of casualties in the kind of unit to which I was likely to be posted was very low indeed. No attempt to talk about God, let alone to con me into coming to his church services – I wasn't within a million miles of that at the time. What he offered me was simply a caring, human response to a young adult's fear of dying almost before the excitement of life had begun.

In the town of Kure there was a small Japanese protestant church. Very small. It looked as if it was struggling. I went in only once to have a look round. Outside, for all to see, was a Christian cross. I had been confirmed at the age of thirteen or fourteen and like so many young people had left the church almost immediately afterwards. But somewhere deep down was a recognition both in talking to the chaplain and also in the little church in Kure, that in some way I already belonged to a family which I could rejoin, without recrimination, at any stage, and that wherever I was in the world, I would be able to find other members who belonged to that same family.

I eventually came back alive and well to England and Oxford, worked in management for some years, became a Christian once more and was subsequently ordained. In those heady days of the 1960s I got swept into a belief that I was there to fill up my church. I guess I had my own personal decade, or nearly two decades, of evangelism! In the first parish of which I was the vicar the communicant figures increased by 100 per cent in seven years; in the second by 90 per cent in the following seven years. I had forgotten very largely the lesson that army chaplain had quietly tried to teach me, that the church was, in those famous words of William Temple, the only society in the world which exists for the sake of those who are not its members. I had also forgotten the silent lesson of the Kure church, that Christianity was more about belonging to a family than about 'going to church'.

In my later years of ministry I have tried to make amends for all this by trying, instead, to meet people where they are, to respond to what may be worrying them, rather than trying to get them to 'come to church'. The fact that this has still seemed to result in more people beginning to come to church might satisfy some, but for me it now became incidental. I was happy when people came to church, but it was not my main concern. This also took away from me a lot of the pressures which often afflict clergy to the end of their lives.

I have also come to realise that over the centuries, when the church has been numerically weak or under persecution it has generally been at its best; when it has been numerically strong it has been at its arrogant worst and has sometimes persecuted others. As Jesus made clear, the church does not exist to be the whole, but to be the leaven or yeast which activates the whole. Not all those who heard Jesus became apostles or even disciples, but I do believe that in some way their lives and the kinds of decisions they made were changed perhaps by a single meeting with him.

So getting people to come to church is not the be-all and end-all of the Christian enterprise. But that does not excuse those who are responsible for the arrangement of church services from struggling week-by-week to make them relevant to where people are and to address their immediate as well as their ultimate concerns. It does not excuse us from trying to offer the best we can to God nor from trying to create a sense of 'otherness'. Hopefully this will echo profound experiences people have had in the world so that they can relate that personal experience to the reality of God.

When people, sometimes after many years as practising Christians, come to me with questions like the one at the start of this chapter, I find I want to try to help them to learn to stay with people where they are rather than feeling that our prime task in life is to put bottoms on pews. We have a more exalted task than that! As the question is expressed, it seems to be as much to do with the embarrassment of the questioner about what goes on in church as with their concern for others. It is a concern I recognise in myself when I have attended quite dreadful services and agonised over what on earth an outsider coming to church for the first time would make of it all.

While again not trying to excuse the mediocrity and irrelevance of much that can happen in church services, is it possible that the questioner has changed? I'd want to explore just what it was that drew him or her into the life of the church in the first place. Was it something to do with profound questions about the meaning and purpose of life? Could it possibly be that as we continue in the Christian life, and maybe become a little more secure in it, we cease to ask those basic questions which actually draw people in the first instance and concentrate instead on lesser questions?

What drew you in the first place into the life of the church? Have you changed? Only this morning I asked a priest whose views are very much on the move, just what it was that drew him into the life of the church in the first place. His response was startlingly similar to my own feeling all those years ago, of wanting to *belong* to something, of wanting to find a place where he mattered, a place where people cared about him and where he had a role, in this case as an altar server. 'What was it that drew you in the first place?' is a good question to ask of those who now feel to some extent disillusioned, maybe not with the church as a whole, but at least with church services.

If for some it is the need to belong, to be recognised, to feel that we matter to other people and to God, for others it will be those ultimate questions. Someone once said to me, 'Once upon a time I used to ask this, this and this . . . but I realise I now no longer ask those questions.'

As we consider what goes on in church services, it may be that those same services are responding in some way to those questions which the outsider is asking, and which we could all usefully go on asking:

- What is the purpose of my life?
- What am I here for?
- Who is God?
- Who am I?

– Where can I feel I belong?
– Where can I feel I *matter*?

I am reminded of the famous story of St Francis in which a brother wanted to know how Francis prayed, the assumption being that Francis prayed aloud. The brother went and crouched outside Francis' cell, and all through the night the prayer of Francis he overheard was just two questions: 'Who are you, God?' and 'Who am I?' I find that story immensely reassuring in that the great St Francis was still asking those absolutely basic questions well on in his life. It's also a challenge to me to go on asking of God and of myself those basic questions which I fear all too many Christians have stopped asking because they think they already know the answers and can pass them on to others. The truth is that we *all* need to remain questioners to the end of our lives . . . 'Who are you, God? . . . Who am I?'

To the extent that going to church is about belonging, feeling valued and wanted and listened to, the individual Christian has a vital role to play. Maybe our friends and acquaintances are not ready – might in some instances never be ready – to join in public worship. This puts the onus back on individual lay Christians to be the church to that person, to be ready to listen to their story and to interpret that story where they can. Christians are all too ready to push this task back on to the clergy, failing to realise that it is a shared task.

I am deeply committed these days to what is rather grandly called a ministry of spiritual direction. I can do this only in the knowledge that it is not I who am the director, but the Holy Spirit. Two people sit down together to try to listen more carefully to the Holy Spirit, the true spiritual director. What is needed is a church where lay Christians are able to listen to others in an attitude of prayer, sometimes to interpret, sometimes to offer suggestions, sometimes simply to be silent. I also believe that we can only carry out this kind of ministry effectively if we ourselves are open enough to be able to share our own story, our own concerns, with someone else who is willing to be our own spiritual director.

Sometimes this kind of talking will lead to our inviting others to come to church with us, whatever the shortcomings of the service. Afterwards we need to be ready to try to answer questions and to accept a measure of incomprehension from the other person. Just as for you and me a very inadequate church service may have inspired us in the early stages, so I think we have to trust that God may speak to others in a similar way.

Think back to your own beginnings, to your own questionings, remembering that God almost certainly worked something for you that was beyond your control and he probably made use of some very inadequate acts of worship!

Can't I be a Christian without going to church?

I have sometimes encountered people who feel themselves so 'out of it' that they would rather be independent Christians – no longer part of an institutional church which seems so remote. We may sometimes feel like this ourselves. A few Saturdays ago my wife and I walked through a nearby town centre and twice encountered strident groups of Christians haranguing passers-by to come to the Lord Jesus Christ to be saved. I experienced for the thousandth time a feeling of revulsion, because that aggressive condemnatory attack was not within a thousand miles of what I understand by Christianity. Conversely, I am quite sure that those people in the market square would not have considered me to be a Christian! They were wanting me to acknowledge that I was a terrible sinner, and that if I did not believe in the Lord Jesus Christ I would assuredly be damned into all eternity.

I have no doubt that those folks honestly believed what they were saying and that they were standing there because they genuinely wanted to save people from being damned into all eternity, but I have a terrible fear that as the Decade of Evangelism proceeds my wife and I may well experience not two but ten embarrassing confrontations when we innocently go shopping. The atmosphere was one of 'whatever you are doing, stop it, because it is sinful: if it's nice and enjoyable, stop it or you will go to hell'.

So here am I, a committed full-time minister of the church, feeling acutely affronted – I would go so far as to say 'violated' – by what some of my fellow Christians are up to. Apart from trading on that neurotic guilt which lies buried in

79

nearly all of us, what on earth would an agnostic passer-by make of it all? What on earth does it mean, to demand of passers-by that they believe in the Lord Jesus Christ and be saved? Who is that Lord Jesus Christ? I suspect he is very different from the one I believe in. What does it mean to the casual passer-by to be saved? For the outsider there is no meaning-content in the jargon. I recall a religious radio broadcast some years ago in which every time a speaker used a bit of religious jargon there was a bleep, just as if that person had used a swear word. It was a powerful way of reminding the speakers how little of what they were saying would be understood by outsiders.

I have every sympathy with the honest, searching, questioning Christian who feels repelled by such public displays. I walked away feeling abused. Did I really want to go on proclaiming to the world that I belonged to all that? That by going on belonging I somehow agreed with it? Would it not be better to opt out and try to live a low-key life of loving and caring outside the institutional church: a life affirming in other people those lovely gifts which God has given to each of us? The more strident and guilt-making some Christians become, the less others will feel they can be a part of it. My example was an extreme one, but the daily press, let alone the religious press, affords numerous examples of embarrassing opinions and actions from Christians.

So there is the heart of the dilemma for an increasing number of people who truly consider themselves to be Christians. Do we say we cannot associate ourselves with so much that goes on in the name of Christianity? That we cannot associate ourselves with the guilt creators? Or do we stay in the church and try to show that Christianity can be different from this?

As I see it at the moment, I want to stay in. For me, to leave would be to show a lack of trust in God. I believe that

God is ultimately guiding us into all truth and that the truth will prevail. The church needs those who continue to search for the truth and who are not content with easy answers. The church desperately needs those who believe that Christianity is life-affirming and liberating rather than creating guilt and dependency.

The operative question is always, 'Do I still consider myself to be a Christian? Do I still see in the gradual, painful, unfolding revelation of God in the Old Testament and in the person of Jesus, a way of living which leads to a greater fulness of life?' As my answer is 'yes' then I believe that I am called to stay in there unless or until someone kicks me out. I believe, then, that those who contemplate leaving the visible church to become what some have called 'independent Christians' would do well to consider two factors.

First, the human need to worship. For most people this means at least at times a corporate activity, being in touch with Something Other *with* others. If we have ever experienced this in our Chrisian life we shall miss it profoundly if we leave. The church may not always manage corporate worship very well, nor will it always be expressing what we might hope it would express, but it is *there*. The poet Thomas Hardy demonstrated the value of corporate worship. A self-proclaimed atheist, Hardy attended church faithfully every Sunday. I do not think we have even begun to understand what meeting to pray together may do for our deeper needs and longings. Our minds – like the poet's – may reject what we hear, but our deeper selves long to belong and to worship.

Second, belonging provides us (or should provide us) with an opportunity to share our views with others, to listen and to be listened to. I find it hard to see how our understanding of God can mature in a balanced way simply by reading and thinking on our own. Christianity is essentially about relationships – relationships with God and relationships with other people. If a Christian community does not provide opportunities for people to share their faith and their doubts with each other it is failing in its duty, and I do have a very real concern for those who find no opportunity of this kind in any church within reasonable distance. It is not always easy to offer them any positive suggestion. For some, regular short stays in retreat houses or with religious communities seem to fill the need which their local churches are failing to meet.

As Christians talk together about their faith they are likely to come alive and to begin to be able to share it with others, not in any embarrassing way but in a way that meets other people where they are. It won't be done in an effort to bludgeon them into a belief system or to warn them of impending damnation, but it will enable them to be open to each other – 'this is how it is for me . . . how is it for you?'

Over the last fifteen years or so, across all denominations, there has been an exciting rediscovery of the value of spiritual direction, spiritual friendship, spiritual guidance.[1] Talking regularly to mature Christians can help us immensely in our Christian journey. For some this may be their only link with the visible church; for others it may be a means of finding their way back again.

Some Christians are confronted by profound dilemmas which may cause them to question their membership of a church. But leaving a church for more superficial reasons is much more common, and in my view much sadder. For example, people don't like the new vicar, priest or minister, or they've had a row with someone or they don't like changes in worship. These are situations which do not involve basic belief, though there may well be some ill-conceived anger at God for 'allowing' this situation to arise.

Each situation needs discussing individually, but it does

distress me that many people are disillusioned with their churches and many clergy are disillusioned with their congregations. I recall an ancient cartoon in which a vicar is saying to his curate, 'Young man – will you please stop referring to the congregation as "the Opposition" '. When people consider leaving a church, careful discussion will frequently bring to the surface an underlying flight-or-fight syndrome: do I go on in the painful situation, fighting all that seems wrong, or do I simply opt out and stop belonging to a Christian community?

A more mature resolution can come about if some course of action can be discovered which is neither flight nor fight. But there may need to be mature Christians around with whom the matter can be discussed in confidence and without pressure to conform. The need for good spiritual directors increases every day.

Reference

1. See details in references to Chapter 1.

Aren't organisations like Friends of the Earth more relevant?

There are a lot of possibilities lurking behind this kind of question. Over the years I have encountered Christians who are up to their ears in churchy organisations and activities. They are either pressed to do more and more by insensitive or guilt-creating clergy or are driven by their own inability to say 'no', which is either a result of their own guilt or an immature reluctance to face confrontation.

Let us imagine that a situation has arisen in which a family moves house and this has given them the chance to rethink their church commitment. People have told me that their church life had become a punitive treadmill with little or no time for their families or for hobbies or recreation. With the move they decided that they simply could not face getting into 'all that' again, and because they found it hard to say 'no', they do not now risk even going to church. At heart they still belong, but a guilt-inducing workaholic ethic in their church has driven them away. They have discovered to their joy and delight that there is more to life than running jumble sales or church committees, that their families need them and that hobbies and mind-stretching interests provide them with a greater fulness of life than that endless round of churchy activities.

In some parts of the church people are made to feel that it is somehow selfish or even sinful to have time for themselves to grow as individuals and simply to enjoy life. I'm afraid that clergy themselves often set a bad example by working far harder than is good either for them or their families, which all too often puts pressure on their congregations to do likewise.

I believe that there is an urgent necessity to recover the concept of the Sabbath as the day (or longer period) of rest. In some church circles the Sabbath means that people labour as hard on a Sunday as they do the rest of the week with church, Bible study groups and prayer meetings. There really is no rest about that kind of a day, no time to stand and stare, no time to loaf and relax and be aware. The true Sabbath of *rest* is very different, according to the Old Testament understanding of one day in the week and occasional longer periods. A true Sabbath might not even entail any involvement with 'church', but be a matter of doing the next thing that comes to hand with as much awareness and relaxedness as possible and pausing whenever it seems right to do so.

The questioner may have had a bad time with the church, and despite having broken loose may still have a conscience and a concern for others. This may be a concern about ecology and conservation, so once the family have moved house they join something like Friends of the Earth or Save the Children. But while people *can* be heavily committed to ecological concerns or the fight against poverty, by and large these will not 'take over' in the same way as excessive church commitments. There is space for other things.

There may indeed be a more caring and accepting spirit in the new concern than they previously found in their church, though here, I think, a measure of caution is necessary. If I am disillusioned with some organisation I am likely to become particularly sensitive to the faults and failings of that organisation, and at least partially deaf to its good qualities. If I move to another organisation, which may only be a move to a different church congregation, it is almost inevitable that I shall be very open to its good points (at least at first) and indulgent towards its weaknesses. I need, after all, to bolster up the rightness of my own free choice! The atmosphere in a secular charity may indeed be more Christian than in some church congregations, but we shall be wise to suspend judgement until we are nearer the centre of the thing. There are, sadly, few human organisations without divisions and power struggles which may become apparent only at a later stage. The closer one moves to the centre of any organisation, Christian or secular, the more one realises the lust for power and authority and control. My own very modest experience of middle-management in the church was a deeply saddening one of seeing good Christians corrupted by a desire for power, status or achievement.

I doubt whether there are many secular oganisations which are very different. In Plato's ideal republic the best people governed to prevent the less good taking over. But how is this to be achieved? Might it be more to do with relinquishing control? Churches don't have to try to run everything themselves; they can quietly allow Christian views to be expressed through an increasing Christian involvement in secular organisations. A quiet restraining voice on the margins is surely better than an urge to control.

The aim is to be Christians in the world rather than drawing people *out* of the world into endless church-based activities. The church would then become a focus for worship, and for teaching and supporting people in their involvement with the structures of the world where they play their part in bringing about God's kingdom.

It cannot be denied that there are very angry and divided churches. My hunch is that these are frequently churches which are guilt-creating and work-obsessed and which have taught a sin-and-redemption theology at the cost of an affirming and balancing teaching on the goodness of creation in general and human potential in particular. If the questioner belongs to an unbalanced sin-and-redemption church, the all-important counterbalance may be found in the life-affirming world of ecology. In a more broadly-based church such a move might not have been necessary.

This brings us back to the recurrent dilemma of whether to stay with an unhappy and uncomfortable situation (either a local church or the wider church). Do we do what we can to heal it, or do we feel we can no longer cope and have to go elsewhere? There is a real question of discernment here. I believe that at most times the body of the church is there for us to serve it and work for the kingdom – in other words to *give*. But there are times in our lives, times of stress and weakness, when we have little to give and need to *draw* strength and support from the body of the church. If that support is not forthcoming it may well be right to look for that support elsewhere, either in a different congregation or further afield.

Conversely, however, there are those who seem to think that the church exists solely to provide them with support at all times and have little awareness of the call to serve. That aspect needs watching: I have sat for hours with people who have grumbled about their church and seemed totally deaf to any suggestion that they themselves might be called to make some effort to change it. Or they might simply be called to stay with a difficult situation to try and work for a more balanced and caring Christian community.

It is very easy for Christians to expect the dynamics of a Christian organisation to be totally different from those in a secular organisation, that all 'should' be sweetness and light. Yet we take into our church life the same selfish selves that we carry around in our work and our families and we also take our own inner fantasies. There is therefore bound to be conflict in church life just as anywhere else. One might hope that the spirit in which opposing views are voiced and heard would be different, but conflict will be there just the same. Christians have a great deal to learn about the constructive use of conflict both as a means of growth and as a way of reaching more balanced and mature decisions which take into account the differences between people. Perhaps one could even learn to rejoice in those differences!

So I should want to ask how far the questioner is able to face up to her or his own anger and negativity and to express it appropriately in appropriate places. Is that anger pushed below the surface in resentment towards an organisation (the church) which then needs to be 'punished' for the discomfort it has caused, by that person leaving it? There are a lot of games which people play which may need exploring. I'd want to find out whether or not the questioner has unrealistic expectations of church life, and whether or not they might grow by staying and struggling and trying to discern what the Holy Spirit might be wanting in order for that place to be healed and to grow.

The question might be obscuring another possibility. Could this person be transferring on to the church anger or disillusion which rightly belongs somewhere else? I was brought up in a clergy household. I was not particularly pressured into any kind of belonging, but the fact that my father was the rector of the parish committed me to being inextricably intertwined with the church. I'm sure it was partly this sense of being trapped which led me to disillusion and subsequently to ten years as a happy pagan.

I also recall a woman deeply involved (not to say enmeshed) in church activities. Her husband was very angry with the church which had effectively taken his wife away from him. It was only when his wife left him that it became clear that he was making the church a scapegoat for the unhappiness in his marriage. With his wife away from him he lost his disillusion with the church and became a faithful and valued member.

How complicated it all is. Few questions or statements are as straightforward as they seem at first. We may well play games with ourselves, refusing to see hidden agendas and deeper underlying questions. So when people talk to us about important matters it is vital that we do not attempt to offer immediate answers, but instead search for the real meaning of the question and help people to discover their own answers which are true for them – at least for the time being.

Why don't Christians think alike on political issues?

Or to put the question in another way, 'Why doesn't the church make up its mind and speak out firmly on this or that issue?' One hears this kind of unhappiness expressed so often. Archbishops find themselves in an impossible situation. If they remain silent on the issue they will be accused of indecision or cowardice; if they speak out they are sure to be greeted with protests. So do we really want 'the church' (in whatever form) to speak out only in a way which accords with our own views?

I do not wish to underestimate the depth of genuine conviction which has led many people to leave the mainstream churches because of their views on nuclear disarmament, for instance, or because the place of women in society and in the church has not been fully endorsed by the whole church. But there is a different question to be asked: 'How fully do I require my own views to be held by the church if I am to remain a member of it? Can I stay in a church which remains silent or even in some cases opposes the views I hold to be desperately important?'

We are here considering 'social and political issues', and there are some Christians for whom this would not be a question. They see the church as otherworldly and concerned only to draw people *out* of the world into the haven of the church to await the end of a sinful world and the separation of sheep from goats in a last judgement before the elect go to eternal joy in heaven.

If we take the Old Testament and the New Testament as a unity, such a position of total unconcern about the structures of this world is untenable. The prophets were highly political people. Moses and the judges were lawgivers and orderers of society in the name of God. For them there was no such thing as 'secular society': everything was the concern of God. It was in this tradition that Jesus told us to pray 'Your will be done *on earth* as it is in heaven'. His will can be done on earth only when the social and political structures of the world enable people to carry out the will of God in security and freedom.

If I thought that the church as a whole was meant to be unconcerned with the reforming of society I know that I, too, would have to leave. But the questioner may have encountered some 'escapist' views of the church, been upset by them and need reassurance that the vast majority of Christians see this world as the place where they are to work for the coming of God's kingdom. This is not to deny our ultimate destination, but to cherish and value the world which God created, which he saw was very good and which he loves and wishes to see transformed. In that transformation we all have a part to play.

It is more likely, however, that the questioner is disillusioned by the variety of views and the apparent indecisiveness of the church. It may be worth discussing with them the question of the catholicity or universality of the church. If the church is for all people, then there will be Christians at various stages along the road of belief and commitment, all continuing to work out just how their faith is best expressed in the world. The more catholic or more universal we are, the wider the variety of views we shall need to be able to tolerate. Even those who seem to want to disconnect from the world may have their place in reminding those who are fully committed to an incarnational, this-world faith, that there is also the dimension of the holiness, transcendence and otherness of God which we lose at our peril. It is, as always, a case of both/and rather than either/or. We lose either side of the paradox to our cost.

The questioner may also fear conflict, wanting a church of happy like-minded people, undisturbed by controversy. As I suggested in the previous chapter, conflict and a hammering out of different points of view may be the best way of finding solutions which match the great variety of personality types and social situations in the world. We all have issues which we believe to be very important. It may indeed be our vocation to work for these, but we shall do well to remember that different issues are the vital ones for other people and our own key issues may be less important for them. We have only a limited amount of energy and we need to be selective about the issues to which we devote that energy.

I believe that individual Christians may have a call to pursue specific issues with all the energy at their command, but without necessarily expecting the church as a whole to endorse their concerns to the same degree. If their concern is rightly placed, their views will eventually very probably prevail, otherwise they will wither away. For the institutional church to speak out as if it were united on issues on which it is obviously divided is to court further unnecessary division. We have to accept that if the church has any claim to be catholic then there will, for example, be Christians of all political parties within that church. We may find it hard to see how Christianity is compatible with one or the other end of the political spectrum. But is it not desirable that the church should contain Christians of all parties in the hope that each will try to persuade their party to take a more Christian stance? Because of the great diversity of Christian opinion the history of specifically 'Christian' political parties in the West has not been encouraging. A not dissimilar dilemma has faced the 'Greens': do they form their own minority party or would they be wiser not to form a specific party but do all they can to influence other political parties in the areas which particularly concern them?

While I abhor those politicians who tell Christians to keep out of politics and stick to 'saving souls' (whatever that may mean) there is a real question as to how far it is right for Christian leaders to attempt to prescribe the detail of any political programme. There are certain general principles which I believe the church needs to state and restate, but the way in which those general principles should be worked out in practical detail is more a matter for individual Christians with specific skills in economics or the social sciences. And even here there will be plenty of scope for honest difference of opinion.

It is all too easy to want to solve complex problems with simplistic solutions, which can only do harm in the long run. One can understand the impatience of the questioner, and maybe the institutional church has been silent for too long on some issues. But in Britain over the last few years the churches have been increasingly bold in opposing many changes in society and have been fiercely reviled by those in power for doing so.

One of the underlying assumptions of this book is that the truth is elusive and it takes hard work to find it. It is all too easy to become impatient and prematurely throw in the towel and leave the church. Yet we remind ourselves again and again that 'A thousand ages in thy sight are like an evening gone'. That is not an argument for supine inactivity, but for faithful perseverance, when at times it seems that all the cards are stacked against us.

Years ago I recall seeing in the financial column of my daily newspaper the wise advice, 'Start from the premise that there is no justice in this world, and you will then be able to campaign without bitterness'. If the church is a home for sinners and not an exhibition of saints we shall have to live with a measure of frustration when the institutional church does not immediately live up to our expectations.

When I was still at school I listened to a radio reconstruction of a medieval disputation. The form of the disputation had very strict rules which I cannot now recall, but in essence it eschewed the somewhat childish approach to argument we usually see today. The approach nowadays is totally confrontational and usually generates more heat than light (as in the House of Commons). The medieval proposer made a statement in favour of a point of view; the opposer did not simply disagree but went as far towards agreement with the proposal as possible: 'With that and that I agree . . . but that and that I deny, because . . .' The proposer would then go as far as possible in agreeing with the other side before turning to what he would deny. In other words the purpose was not confrontational but a *narrowing down* of the area of disagreement in order to struggle towards the truth.

According to strict rules of logic a point would be reached where one side or the other would concede defeat, but in a limited area. Now while we might be doubtful today about the reality or sufficiency of such rules of logic, it seems to me that this narrowing down and searching for as much agreement as possible is a very civilised and very *Christian* way of going about things. I wish the church could set an example by returning to it. There is too the equally Christian approach of the Society of Friends who sit in prayer and silence with the occasional word until a common mind is reached.

Part Four

QUESTIONS ABOUT LIVING

QUESTION 16

Why are Christians so obsessed with sin?

Many older Christians – and among them some who have concluded that they are no longer Christians – will recall little books of self-examination which they were expected to work through before receiving Holy Communion. In those dreadful little books the whole gamut of possibilities for sin seemed to be raised, especially anything to do with 'impurity', by which it was meant, I always felt, any glimmering of awareness that God had created us as sexual beings. Such was the general tenor of the questioning that it seemed to be assumed one was guilty of all of them. To say, even to oneself, that one was not guilty of even a few sins was an act of culpable pride and therefore yet another sin.

We were locked into sin and guilt. God might graciously forgive us, but such was our universal condition of innate sinfulness that when we got out our little book again the following week we had to go through the same dismal process all over again. It became clear that God had us under his almighty thumb for ever, and we must remain prostrate before him in pathetic and grovelling gratitude. It was an act of enormous condescension that we might be forgiven at all, for had we not crucified Jesus ourselves? Even our smallest sin seemed to be enough to crucify Jesus. By some appalling celestial chemistry, the fact that I had failed to return my school-friend's ruler or india-rubber had hammered the nails through the hands of Jesus.

This is not, unfortunately, an attitude confined to young children. Try this prayer of Tanqueray (c.1930) for size:

> May I know thee, O Lord, that I may love thee; may I
> know myself that I may despise myself.

This, as I know from countless hours of talking with people,
is no exaggeration of how the Christian religion is frequently
experienced; it is the staple diet of many evangelistic services, and one can still hear sermons in which this is the
underlying theology . . . a self-hatred which is truly sick. We
have to be made to feel wicked and sinful in order that God
may forgive us, but we are also reminded that since we are
innately sinful we shall always sin and always have to remain
in that kind of grovel before God.

There are people who come to talk to me who have exam-
ined their consciences carefully and while realising that there
is always room for improvement – certain areas which need
attention – they have come to the thoughtful conclusion that
there is no cause for them to grovel before God as miserable
sinners. They have come in a frame of mind which has
recognised God at work in themselves and in others, they
have the privilege of sharing in God's work in the world, and
have been given many talents and abilities which they enjoy
using in the service of God and of others.

I can detect no pride or smugness in this when I hear it;
rather an adult awareness of gratitude and a call to use their
gifts. However, some clergy would respond to this by reminding their visitor that they were really guilty of the sin of
pride: that there is a great gulf between God and ourselves,
and we are all part of fallen human nature. God possesses an
unutterable holiness and purity beside which we are
wretched and unclean and Jesus died on the cross for the sins
of everyone. And so on.

I totally agree that the holiness of God lies beyond our
utmost imagining, but I also believe that countless Christians
have been crippled and kept in infantile dependency by this

obsession with sin and guilt which also serves so well to uphold the assumed authority of those in ecclesiastical power. This is especially apparent where the power of forgiveness appears to be confined to priestly absolution rather than to the love of God. I believe that far more Christians suffer from a disablingly low self-image, encouraged by the church, than suffer from the sin of pride. I do not believe we can even begin to 'die to ourselves' unless we *have* a self which we love and value and cherish. Without loving and respecting our self (loving our neighbour *as* ourselves) there *is* nothing there to die or to give away.

As in all spiritual direction and counselling I believe it is important to start where each person is. I believe that every Christian would benefit from talking with another person from time to time about their sins, failures and weaknesses and in that context to be reminded of God's love and forgiveness. I also believe in the value and importance of confession because to go and talk with another human being before God in confession presses us to think carefully about uncomfortable things which most of us would prefer to push under the carpet. But I also believe that when people come to talk about their sins, failures and weaknesses, we need equally to talk together about the gifts and talents God has given them so that they may value themselves and begin to see more clearly what role God may be wanting them to fulfil in the world – the way that they can use these gifts and abilities to the full and thus become themselves.

Better still, if we can begin with gifts and talents we are more likely to get the sins and weaknesses into proportion and to realise that we do not have to carry the whole weight of the world on our own shoulders and that some of the things we feel responsible for are a shared responsibility or part of our heredity or our environment. Those with an introverted personality are more prone than extroverts to take this great weight upon themselves; extroverts are more likely to blame others, introverts tend to be 'intra-punitive', extroverts 'extra-punitive'.

This is not to deny sin or a measure of personal responsibility, but to affirm those words of Jesus which cannot be repeated too often, 'I call you no longer servants but friends' (John 15.15). Our proper attitude before God is not one of grovelling but of standing upright, confident of the friendship and the gifts we have been given.

Nor is this to deny an awareness of corporate sin. Our confession of sin is not only personal sin. We each carry a portion of responsibility for the awful mess that humanity has made of God's world and its scandalous inequality. We know we could all have done more to care or protest or campaign.

Nevertheless, a great deal of spiritual direction has to do with releasing people from heavy guilt, especially where this continues to be laid upon them by some sections of the church, keeping them in a permanent kind of bondage, however much they may proclaim that they are 'saved' or 'born again'. If only we could get sin and guilt into proportion with gifts and grace, I believe many who have ceased to consider themselves Christians would realise not only that they have belonged all the time, but that their faith is healthier and more mature than they have been taught.

Does being a Christian always mean putting others first?

I believe this is probably the most central and difficult issue Christianity is facing at the present time; how to strike a balance between self-denial and the affirmation of life.

At first sight the questioner seems to be doubting the very clear command of Jesus himself that we should deny ourselves, take up our cross and follow him. Christianity has a long tradition of asceticism. The wonderful wisdom of the Desert Fathers was accompanied by a massive mortification of the flesh, with a belief that this maltreatment of the flesh was good in itself, keeping oneself more or less permanently in a state of desperate hunger. Many years ago I recall reading in a retreat house a very ancient biography of the Curé d'Ars which viewed with unconcealed admiration the fact that the Curé had lived for a week on a few mouldy potatoes. There seemed to me at the time to be something quite sick about this, yet it is the kind of thing which runs throughout Christian history.

I should like to balance this ascetic concept, which treats the human body as a battleground for heroic self-denial, with the equally theological idea of stewardship. God has given us our bodies as vehicles through which we are enabled to serve him. We should not think of maltreating a piece of machinery by failing to oil it or service it or keep it in good condition: to do so would be sheer irreponsible waste. The human body is no different. It is there to be treated with care and honour and given the food and exercise it needs to enable it to function as well as possible in God's service. It seems to me that we owe this to God. This does not exclude the use of carefully controlled fasting or dieting in order to improve our health or sharpen our minds. Similarly, I see no virtue in being cold if our minds then cease to function properly. Surely we should treat our bodies in such a way as to make them as ready as possible to serve God.

Is it not once more a matter of *balance* – a balance of self-denial on the one hand and concern to be fit and active on the other?

But there are many forms of self-denial. It has been claimed that there have been more Christian martyrs in our own century than in all the previous nineteen centuries put together. Brave people become martyrs when there are causes or principles to defend or people to stand up for. To deny oneself or even to face martyrdom for the sake of people or a cause is very different from a constant self-denial just for the sake of it. The first is life-affirming – affirming the importance of people or principles or causes; the second is life-denying.

I do not see Jesus as a person who denied life. He seems to have had a sense of fun, to have had many friends and followers, and to have enjoyed life. His illustrations and metaphors were not about denying life, but about ordinary everyday things and most of all about feasts and weddings. It is some of his later followers who have turned this affirmation of life into a denial of life.

Bishop Stephen Verney, in his early book *Fire in Coventry*,[1] put forward an order of priorities which I have found extremely helpful over the years. I have always regretted it when I failed to observe them. The first priority is prayer. The second priority is time off: time every day for recreation or being with friends or family; a day of recreation each week, and a longer period for holidays. Then and only then, do we say that the rest of our time is there in which to serve God. We cannot give away or even 'deny' if there is no real self *to* give away or deny.

How, then *do* we understand the idea of self-denial if we acknowledge that life is to be enjoyed and affirmed, that we need time for our families, our friends and ourselves, that we need to be whole people with leisure pursuits to keep us alive and interesting people, that our bodies are there to be cared for even better than we should care for a fine piece of machinery?

Is it not a matter of *attitude*? Am I denying myself in a blanket kind of way because the gospels apparently tell me to do so, or am I denying myself some good thing because I am genuinely concerned about others? Even here one needs to tread cautiously. Am I serving others in a sacrificial way because I need to be needed, or because I get a kick out of it, or because I want to be the saviour of other people, or because I want to exercise my skills on someone else? Human motivation is infinitely devious, and it is salutary to bear in mind the old saying that you know when people are being 'done good to' by the hunted look on their faces!

Or again, what is the *spirit* in which some act of self-denial is being carried out? Is it joyful, or angry and resentful? Some Christians who deny themselves a great deal in order to serve others go around with barely suppressed anger or resentment. 'It's all being left to me,' they seem to be saying angrily, 'Why aren't you doing as much as me?' Yet others may have a very different outlook on life. The things they consider important may be different, and they may well be making sacrifices in other areas of life which they consider to be more important.

I am sure that it is the *attitude* rather than the *achievement* which is important. I would rather go without help than be given it grudgingly. Self-denial all too easily results in a spin-off of superiority towards others, a latter-day Pharisaism.

Would it be better to suggest that self-denial is not a way of life as such, because it then becomes not only *self*-denying but *life*-denying, but rather to hold that in the course of our journey through life there will be people, principles or causes which we believe we are called to fight and campaign for sacrificially? So it is caring and loving which are the true motives, not abstract self-denial as a principle in itself. For a good cause or for a person there may be almost infinite degrees of *healthy* self-denial, and one marvels at some of today's martyrs in South America, in Africa, almost anywhere in the world. This is life-affirming self-denial in a worthy cause.[2]

The other principle which I believe lies behind a healthy view of self-denial is that of non-attachment. Yet here again it is so easy for non-attachment to be understood in a negative life-denying way, as if it means that we can't enjoy anything. There have been eminent and highly regarded Christians over the centuries who regarded it as sinful even to laugh; merriment was seen as totally unsuitable for the Christian. I do not think we should gloss over these unpalatable facts, but bear them in mind as horrible warnings as to how Christianity can be distorted. Every age has its own distortions.

A healthy view of non-attachment means that we can enjoy to the full the good things which come our way; to do otherwise would be to be ungrateful to God. Things go wrong when we come to see those good things as a 'right' to which we are entitled, or when we cling to them, depend on them, or regard them as our security instead of trusting in God. To the extent that we are truly non-attached, we find pleasure and delight in the good things which come our way. But we shall be ready to let go, to 'deny ourselves' without clinging if they are taken from us. In the final analysis each one of us stands naked and alone before God, however rich and rewarding our lives and relationships may be. I suspect that the ultimate confrontation with God at the end of our lives will be less painful if we have been prepared to 'let go' of some of the good things which we cling to so readily. We shall enjoy what is given without clinging and be ready to give it up if people or good causes demand this.

So much for theory; but theory needs refining and working out in the decisions of everyday life. When people talk about self-denial there is usually some specific situation which will have brought them to raise this question. To that specific situation we may be able to bring some of the points raised here. Is it self-denial for its own sake, or for the sake of some deeper self-aggrandisement? Is it rooted in pride or in the need to control others, to be their 'saviour'? Is it a neurotic response to a punishing super-ego, or is it motivated by guilt which needs to be assuaged? Is it perhaps a denial of the goodness of the bodies God has given us? Or is the proposed self-denial a true response to the needs of others? Is it motivated by love for others or by a deep concern for a cause or a principle?

In actual practice I believe it is, mercifully, not too difficult to distinguish good self-denial from bad self-denial. In the final analysis we might ask whether it is life-affirming for others as well as for ourselves, or is it simply a response to our own perceived needs and of no use to other people?

References

1. Stephen Verney, *Fire in Coventry* (1964)
2. See, for example, Sheila Cassidy, *Good Friday People* (Darton, Longman and Todd 1990)

Why do I always feel guilty about the Third World?

In one form or another this is a cry of anguish which very many of us have raised at one time or another and perhaps go on raising. Perhaps there is an element of anger at a God who 'allows' this kind of suffering, so we might first need to consider the question in the light of what we believe about God. Do we envisage God as totally omnipotent yet criminally inactive, or as a God whose freedom to act is circumscribed by the freedom given to human beings? Do we see God as also engaged in a developing world with all the pains and strife of growing?

This is not only a question for Christians but for *all* human beings. Christian and non-Christian alike suffer from troubles of conscience over their own comfort when there is so much suffering and deprivation in the world. If our consciences are sensitive we may find that however simply we live we still feel guilty and privileged. The only logical conclusion may then be to go and share the life of the poorest of the poor. Some dedicated Christians have done just this, for example, the Little Brothers and Sisters of Charles de Foucauld who live on the same wages and in the same conditions as the poor in the big cities of the world.

When this question comes my way I find it better to admit frankly at the beginning that it is one with which I continue to struggle myself and I have yet to discover a way of living with it which satisfies my own conscience. I think it is important for us to be able to acknowledge that there are some questions which we have to continue to struggle with together to find even a tentative and temporary way of living with them. We are thus able to share a common unhappiness which I believe to be the only honest way.

Could it be that the extent of our simplicity of life is a matter of individual vocation, or is to say that a cop-out? Might we perhaps ask, 'Does the course of action you propose, this simplicity of living you have in mind, seem to be where God is calling you? Is this course of action primarily motivated by guilt or by concern?' To see this as a matter of individual vocation would at least avoid our being judgemental about others. I am aware that some Christians whom I greatly respect live more lavishly than I do, while others live with a frugality which worries me. But who am I to pass judgement either way? God may have a different path for them.

Maybe this is one of those areas of life where it is right and necessary that we feel a constant pressure to go on reviewing the way we live and the generosity with which we live. Perhaps this is the constant, subtle pressure of God upon us? Maybe it is a *developing* vocation so that as we become more committed Christians we are called to live with a simplicity which would not previously have been possible for us? If so, this suggests a progression which is the reverse of much that we see around us. Usually, as people become established in their professions, and children leave home, their lifestyle gradually becomes more lavish and self-indulgent. Jesus pointed to this when he warned the rich man who was about to take his ease that his soul would be demanded of him that very night. This sounds not a million miles away from the middle-aged executive's heart attack?

If people come to us with this sense of guilt about their lifestyle, we might do well to look out for the extent to which it might be a neurotic guilt. Someone once came to me suggesting that he should never again go out for a meal, have a holiday or go to the cinema because a relative who lived on the other side of the world was unemployed and would not be able to afford to do these things. This sounded like a denial which would have assisted no one; its only effect would have been to diminish an already restricted life. Simplicity of life surely should not mean narrowness of life.

Those who have lived and worked in Third World countries often point out that what we may perceive as deprivation does not seem to prevent people living with a greater sense of joy and fun than is found in affluent countries, as they take a delight in the smallest and simplest things. Clearly we have much to learn from them. Fulness of life is not to be defined by degrees of affluence. Nonetheless this should not blind us to the fact that there are scandals of grinding poverty not only overseas but much nearer home which cry out for action.

We might helpfully look at our response to Third World issues in terms of exploring just what are the particular gifts God has given to us. How can each one of us be of most use in alleviating suffering? For some, the Mother Teresas of this world, the call will be to live alongside the poor in a similar poverty while at the same time drawing the attention of others to that suffering. For those with different gifts, it may be more a matter of working to change the structures of society so as to eradicate these scandals. For others there may not be a call to direct action, but to indirect work, raising moral issues through the medium of painting, music, drama or literature. Some people are called to enhance our vision, our sense of fun and the quality of life for all. For those with artistic gifts there are many indirect ways in which they may be called to serve the needy of the world. It may then be a matter of constantly questioning our way of life and searching for the specific ways in which our own particular gifts may be used to alleviate the misery of the world.

Most people receive more cries for help from genuine

charities than could possibly be answered. I sometimes suggest to people that they would do well to select one or two concerns to which to give their support. If they give and work as hard as they can for their chosen concerns, these can be allowed to stand for all the others which they cannot support. If we all responded to the moving of the Spirit, there would probably be such a spread of good works that all areas of need would be covered.

The question of world poverty and suffering is one where Christians can and should work alongside those of all faiths and those of none in a common concern for a humanity. But I do not see that it helps anyone if we also decide to abandon the church in anger against God or in a vain hope of avoiding a sense of guilt. As in all things, I believe that attitude and motivation are important and that these should be positive, caring and hopeful, rather than negative and guilt-ridden.

Might there be some value in looking at the concept of sacrifice, not a popular theme these days, even among Christians? The word 'sacrifice' has acquired a negative connotation and is primarily seen as 'giving up'. Today we sacrifice with regret: 'We cannot afford a car any longer – we'll have to sacrifice it.' In this context the word simply means giving something up. However, in Old Testament times a sacrifice was regarded in a far more positive way.

Today the concept of sacrifice is wholly secular, for example 'actress sacrifices mink coat'. In Old Testament times a sacrifice was wholly religious.

Today sacrifices are not offered *to* anyone. We simply sacrifice something: in the Second World War Winston Churchill just called for sacrifices. In the Old Testament sacrifices were always offered *to* God.

Today a sacrifice is usually as small as possible: something we try to avoid. In the Old Testament a sacrifice was as large and expensive as possible and offered with *joy*, as I believe the costly ointment on the feet of Jesus was offered with joy. In much the same spirit we give presents to our children and to those we love which cost more than we can afford, with a similar joy.

Today when we speak of sacrifice, the main emphasis is on giving up and a *loss*; in Old Testament times the main emphasis was on the giving. The loss was not the essential point: a sacrifice was more a kind of present, a sacrifice *to* the Lord. Our concentration today is on ourselves, the givers, whereas then it was a concentration on the Lord to whom it was given.

I believe that it makes a great deal more sense of our own sacrifices if we see them in this light of offering something good to God; and it also makes a great deal more sense of the sacrifice of Jesus on the cross. Sacrifice becomes a kind of thanksgiving, or eucharist, for God's gifts to us. In the Old Testament people were reluctant to offer God anything which was of little value. My father, who was also a priest, hated jumble sales and condemned them in the words of King David who said, 'Shall I offer to the Lord that which costs me nothing?' In the Old Testament people offered to God their own valued possessions, because our possessions are a kind of extension of ourselves, and in sacrificing some of their possessions to God the Hebrews felt that they were giving something of themselves back to him, not as a negative gesture, but as an act of thanksgiving.

Could it be that to view our giving to others as a positive, joyful thing, as a giving also to God, might take this whole issue out of being something negative and guilt-filled into something totally different and healthier.

If, as has been suggested, the last bit of ourselves to be converted is our pocket, maybe the extent of our financial sacrifice is a measure of the level of our commitment? If true, it is a salutary thought.

But I go on struggling away with this one and so, I hope, will you.

Why do Christians have so many hang-ups about sex?

As I have already said, some of my time is spent in running courses to help both laity and clergy in the ministry of spiritual direction. Over the years we have found that issues of sexuality give rise to considerable anxiety not only in those who come to talk, but in the directors themselves.

There is frequently a conflict between the traditional teaching of the church and what people have experienced or have encountered in their own families. It is particularly hard for clergy who feel under pressure to proclaim traditional Christian views on sexuality from the pulpit, but who may have irregular situations within their own congregations and families. Those involved with interviewing potential clergy will be familiar with a very different understanding of sexuality among some younger ordinands. There is thus frequently a gulf between public proclamation and what is said in confidential individual discussion. Small wonder that clergy may experience a loss of integrity while others may accuse them of hypocrisy. The issue is probably at its most acute when bishops have to make decisions regarding clergy whom they know to be practising homosexuals. When does discretion become hypocrisy and when does hypocrisy become discretion? There is a very real dilemma: clergy do not wish to encourage laxity or the trivialisation of sex, and yet they cannot deny that real life may call for compromises.

There has, unfortunately, been a Christian view of sex as inherently nasty or dirty. This blasphemous idea, which denigrates part of God's creation, is fortunately less in evidence these days. But an older questioner might have acquired this idea in earlier years, and may need reassurance that most Christians today have a different understanding of sexuality. More prevalent is a kind of unspoken feeling that God didn't get sexuality quite right. It is primarily seen as a worry and a constant temptation to sin, rather than a gift of God in his creation to be approached with joy and delight.

In some Christian circles there is still the idea that sexuality exists specifically for the purpose of procreation and not really for pleasure. This seems to me to stem from the envy and frustration which can sometimes arise in celibates. Even some married people may acknowledge in honest discussion that they are envious of what a younger generation seems to enjoy without guilt, while they themselves feel they have missed out on something in earlier years.

In the area of sexuality people are sometimes so ferociously condemned that I am astonished they want to stay in the church. I recall some years ago a man coming to me who had happily remarried after a disastrous first marriage. He had recently moved into the diocese and he showed me a letter from his former bishop telling him that as long as his first wife was alive he must never present himself for Communion. Had I been in his position I am sure that I would have been less tolerant than my visitor and would have left the church or simply ignored the bishop's directive. Happily we were able to resolve the situation for him to the satisfaction of his own delicate conscience. But I cannot understand a point of view which would seem to condemn a comparatively young man to spending the rest of his life frustrated and alone when he wants to have his own family. Why do some sections of the church seem ready to forgive almost anything except marital breakdown and remarriage which must remain permanently unforgiven?

Much guilt may surround sexuality for many older Christians. I recall an older woman whose marriage had been

111

physically unsatisfactory but who had had a fulfilling sexual relationship earlier in life. Brought up with traditional Christian views, she had been tormented by guilt about her earlier relationship for years. As we talked, I invited her to lay aside for the moment the moral rightness or wrongness of her earlier relationship and consider whether she had grown because of that relationship and received from it a fulness of life which would have otherwise been impossible. As time went on this woman became able to appreciate the joy and fulfilment of that earlier relationship which had given her a great deal. We can spend too much time looking at 'right' and 'wrong'. Perhaps it is sometimes better to ask whether, under God, a relationship has enabled both parties to grow and to give out to others.

I remember a gathering in which violently condemnatory remarks were being made about homosexuality. As the temperature rose, one man observed quietly, 'I don't think I'd come to any of you lot for help', and he explained how he had been living for many years with another man in a relationship which they expected to continue for the rest of their lives. He spoke of how they had supported each other over the years in times of difficulty, darkness and sickness, and how without his friend's help, he would not have been able to continue. The meeting was remarkably subdued thereafter.

If there were no limitations of confidentiality I could tell many other stories like this, and so could many people. These stories have nothing to do with casual relationships easily abandoned, nor with cruelty or a crude seeking after pleasure, but the relationships concerned would be considered irregular in the light of narrow Christian teaching. Yet they all gave life not only to those involved but to others. And this would not have been possible had the people concerned remained alone.

This is not an argument for 'anything goes'. But when there are people who are battered by narrow orthodoxy, and are thinking of leaving the church, I think it is important to admit to them that there are many Christians who wish to look at each situation in the fullest and broadest way and in the light of the particular circumstances. They may be people whose lives are lived in accordance with the strictest sexual standards but they take the view that it is not appropriate for a spiritual director to sit in judgement on others.

These situations raise the basic question 'Am I still a Christian?' Are we to opt out of the church if our views or conduct are unacceptable to narrower orthodoxies, thus making the church still narrower and more cut off from the lives of the majority of people – a 'sect' church of the kind which I suspect Jesus would have deplored? Or do we stay within the church in order to maintain a balance and a variety of views, in order to be truly catholic (that is to say, universal) and maintain our solidarity with the whole of humanity?

In the parable of the sheep and the goats, Jesus implied some kind of separation or judgement. But it seems to me that Jesus was far more frequently on the side of those whom the narrow-minded called sinners and against those who considered themselves upright and righteous. The gospel calls for love rather than condemnation; and in the context of sexuality condemnation readily springs from envy or sexual frustration.

It is again a question of motivation: is our behaviour motivated by loving and caring, or do we instead exploit others? The church has been all too ready to overlook the 'hard' sins of those in power and authority – greed, lust for power, pride, ambition, selfishness, ruthlessness, lies, envy – yet quick to condemn the sins of softness, the sins of the senses. This imbalance perhaps says something about the

113

character of those who reach the top in the power structures of the church.

The development of the Church of England marriage service is instructive and encouraging. 'Marriage is given', runs the introduction to the order of service in the 1980 Alternative Service Book, 'that with delight and tenderness they may know each other in love, and, through the joy of their bodily union, may strengthen the union of their hearts and lives.' This is a far cry from the grudging negativity of the 1662 Book of Common Prayer which states that marriage 'was ordained for a remedy against sin, and to avoid fornication; that such persons as have not the gift of continency might marry, and keep themselves undefiled members of Christ's body.'

When people are angry about the narrow views of the churches on sexuality I think we may begin by acknowledging that they are right and that narrowmindedness has often been the case in the past. But we need to tell them that there is now a very positive view of sexuality as a means of cementing and enhancing marriage, and not simply as a discreet stratagem for the procreation of children.

We live in a country where there now seems to be an almost universal acceptance of sexual relationships before marriage. I hear younger people saying, 'There isn't a problem; we cannot understand why you older people make such heavy weather of it all.' As one of that older generation myself I listen to what is being said. I do not believe it is for me to comdemn or to sit in judgement. But I do want to go on asking whether anyone is being harmed by these extra-marital relationships. Is sexuality being used in a casual way so that something which could express the specialness, uniqueness and permanence of a relationship is simply trivialised? It has always seemed to me that a full sexual relationship is the means given to us by God to express the specialness of a relationship. It is much more than an expected accompaniment to relationships which may not be very committed, or even casual.

Perhaps, then, when people come to talk, it should be the positive side of relationships which is stressed, and we may need to make it clear that while most Christians now hold positive views of sexuality, this does not mean that for us 'anything goes'.

Why doesn't being a Christian make me more happy?

This seems to me like an extroverted statement. The implication of this question is that it is *God*'s fault that we continue to suffer negative emotions, or even that there's no God to answer our prayers at all. It could be described as 'extra-punitive', that is to say, the blame is being externalised.

An introverted statement would be intro-punitive rather than extra-punitive: 'It's all my fault.' To my existing negative emotions I add the further negativity of feeling guilty. Somehow I 'ought not' as a Christian to be angry/anxious/stressed/depressed, or whatever.

In so far as these are undesirable or unhealthy attributes it has always surprised me that while few Christians have difficulty in accepting that they may contract physical illnesses without any sense of guilt or failure, many find it hard to accept mental illness. God is not usually blamed for rheumatism or appendicitis, nor do we normally blame ourselves for such conditions. One wonders why it should be any harder to understand that just as we may be born with deformed limbs so we may be born with a tendency to depression or a hot temper, or that the events of our lives may lead us to become anxious or stressed.

We can usually see other people's situations far more clearly than our own. Clergy and others who talk to me would be the first to see when someone else was stressed through overwork, yet may be totally unwilling to acknowledge stress from overwork in themselves. Some may be ready enough to grant that they are stressed from overwork but decline to do anything about it. They may even be quite proud to be overworked because this makes them feel needed. Some, indeed, maintain that there is nothing they *can* do to lessen their workload.

Just as physical illness may need a general practitioner, so depression or anxiety may need therapy or counselling. I believe that in physical illness God works through the knowledge and skill of a doctor or nurse and that is the way in which we are usually cured. Why may not God be working equally through the therapist and counsellor? We can hardly hold God responsible if we do not avail ourselves of posible means of cure. I find the suspicion of psychiatrists among some Christians deeply disturbing.

Outside help may well cure or relieve our symptoms, but we may also conclude that we are by nature depressive or anxious and so need to develop strategies for dealing with these feelings. It may be possible to adapt our lifestyle so that such feelings are less likely to occur and there's no doubt that patterns of living can be altered to reduce the level of stress. I see no reason to be shaken in our Christian faith because we may have neurotic symptoms. Few, if any, are totally free of them.

There is plenty of good literature around about dealing with stress but once we have found ways of lessening the stress we need to be aware of the temptation to take on even more work which brings us back again to the original level of stress!

I find it hard to blame God or pronounce him ineffectual when our condition may be the result of heredity, upbringing, workload or lifestyle and when we have done little or nothing to improve matters or discover ways of living with that condition. It could be argued that at the heart of the anxiety position lies a lack of trust in God. We can indeed ask God for more trust, but I do not believe we can simply grit our teeth and will ourselves to have more trust and therefore less anxiety, for trust is a grace, a gift from God.

I think most of us find as we mature that some problems of personality or temperament seem to resolve themselves and no longer trouble us. This means that we have reduced the number of thing we have to struggle with. We know that we may have to struggle for the rest of our lives with, for example, a hot temper. On the other hand perhaps a tendency to envy or uncharitableness will be resolved.

I never tire of the engaging story from the Desert Fathers of Abba John the Dwarf, who prayed to be delivered from the passions. Rather surprisingly he was! By 'the passions' the Desert Fathers did not mean passions for justice or for loving or caring, but the passions of envy, hatred, malice and all uncharitableness. But when John the Dwarf confided this happy result to a senior brother, the brother suggested that he would do better to ask God to give the passions back to him, 'so', he said, 'that you may regain the affliction and humility that you used to have, for it is by warfare and not by deliverance that the soul makes progress.' The better prayer is for strength to fight or endure rather than for deliverance. I find it immensely reassuring that there is a positive content to the negativities which can encourage us to go on working at them.

So as some Christians have seen it – and so often we see things very differently from the rest of the world – our negative emotions may in some strange way be helping us to grow as we continue to work with them. It does not matter – in traditional terms we might say that it is not sinful – if angry or lustful or envious thoughts come to mind, because there's not much we can do about things that just happen. It only matters or becomes sinful if we do or say something which will hurt another person. Much has been written in recent years about it being all right to be angry, even angry with God.[1] But people still come to me feeling guilty about their anger and they are horrified if they discover that they are really angry with God. In spiritual direction much time is spent helping people come to terms with anger in themselves. Yet anger contains a vast reservoir of energy which can be turned to good use in motivating us to fight against all that is wrong in the world, rather than against ourselves, or others, or God.

So instead of blaming *God* for anxiety, depression or anger, if we are extroverts, or blaming ourselves for these emotions if we are introverts, we Christians would do well to 'make friends' with such emotions, and realise that they may help us in the formation of character. Negative emotions can contain useful energy, or be God-given indicators that our lifestyle needs to be changed. In other words, what is that dark emotion trying to tell you?

Reference

1. See, for example, John San ˍˍd, *Evil, the Shadow side of Reality* (New York 1988)

Epilogue — Palm Sunday 1991

I have wondered many times during the drafting of this little book whether it will not seem absurd to many readers to have presumed to take some of the deepest questions facing Chrisitans and others at this time and to give each a few brief pages when a whole book would have been more appropriate for each question. However, not everyone has the time to read twenty books! The intention has not been to presume to offer answers, but rather to suggest a few ways in which we might begin to think positively about these questions, and to encourage others to do so. Many people are going through a period of doubt or of disillusionment with the church, or of wondering whether they are really Christians at all. Some have been driven to doubt by those who pressurise them into thinking that they are not 'proper' Christians unless they hold a particular view of the Bible or the cross, or have had a particular experience of Jesus as their personal saviour. Someone once said dismissively of a number of people whom I regarded as fine Christians that they were 'nice people, but not really Christians'. In other words they did not conform to the speaker's narrow definition of Christianity.

As I write this on Palm Sunday, the day on which we begin to walk once more in the way of the cross, I believe more strongly than ever that there are many different ways of the cross. I do not in any way deny the reality of the experience of some 'born again' Christians or similar groups who enjoy 'absolute certainty'. But I would want to invite them to consider whether they are not still at an early stage of the journey. Might it not be more in keeping with Christian

120

humility to acknowledge that there is far more that we do *not* know?

The way of the cross seems to me to imply struggle, failure, darkness and doubt. It seems to me facile to say that Jesus did this for us and that now everything must be light and joy and jolly guitars. We are called to take up our own cross and follow, and Colossians 1.24 is highly relevant here: 'It makes me happy to be suffering for you now, and in my own body to make up all the hardships that still have to be undergone by Christ for the sake of his body, the church . . .' (NJB).

There are many little resurrections which call for suffering before there can be greater ones. I do not believe that we can come to a true resurrection and a true light, unless we have struggled with the negative elements within us. Those who talk to me in the midst of such struggles usually seem to be closer to God and more humble, more open and more aware than many who claim to have all the answers and want to tell others that they are wrong. In some places it is not easy to find a church where an openness to questions is welcomed. I think that those who consider leaving the church often do so simply because they have not so far been able to find other Christians who think as they do.

In England a recent important move has come in the founding of 'TRUST', which is an attempt to bring together open-minded and questioning Christians.[1]

The first Palm Sunday was a glorious event, a hint of what lay in the future, but in one sense it was a false dawn, for the deepest darkness was yet to come. It is when things are dark that we are tempted to give up the struggle, to leave, to opt out. Of course there is much that is wrong in the church – that is nothing new, but it seems all the more necesary to go on struggling to help that church to resemble more closely the Christ we have begun to know. If the church is to be truly catholic, truly universal, it will need to be much wider than at present, and to encompass a great deal more fearless speculation as we learn new things about the extent and wonder of God's creation.

We began with an image of a jigsaw puzzle and a game of dominoes. For some there will always be a need to try to make coherent sense and wholeness of our experience, a need which we ignore at our peril, the need to complete our personal jigsaw puzzle. But we shall equally be in peril, in danger of losing new truths, unless we are also prepared to follow each line of thought which seems to be true to our experience – to play the game of dominoes – or at the very least, to allow *others* to play that game.

Each of those lines of dominoes, if faithfully and fearlessly followed, will, I believe, lead through a lot of darkness and uncertainty, maybe of hostility and opposition, they but will (if true to our deepest experience) lead to new insights and new glimpses of the way, the truth and the life.

Reference

1. TRUST, 26–30 Tottenham Road, London N1 4BZ.